u - 5.1

Westminster Bones

The Real Mystery of the Princes in the Tower

By
Richard Unwin

By the Same Author

The Laurence the Armourer Series:

On Summer Seas – The Fighting Plantagenets
A Wilderness of Sea – The Rise of King Richard III
The Roaring Tide – A Tale of High Treason

The Doom Assigned – King Richard III in Victory

Other Books:

Who Wrote Marlowe – Christopher Marlowe Exposed
Ironmaster – A Brief History of John Wilkinson

Web Site - www.quoadultra.net

Copyright © Richard Unwin November 2015

Tyrrell

Their lips were four red roses on a stalk,
Which in their summer beauty kiss'd each other.
A book of prayers on their pillow lay;
Which once, quoth Forrest, "almost changed my mind;
But, O, the devil" – there the villain stopped;
When Deighton thus told on: "we smothered
The most replenished sweet work of nature,
That from their prime creation e'er she fram'd."
Hence both are gone with conscience and remorse;
They could not speak; and so I left them both,
To bear this tidings to the bloody king.

Richard III Act IV, scene III.
William Shakespeare

Contents

Introduction

In the year 1674, workmen who were excavating for some building alterations within the Tower of London, were said to have discovered a chest or box containing human bones. They were apparently the remains of two young children aged around twelve and ten years. As they were located in a spot that tradition identifies as possibly the place of burial of the sons of King Edward the Fourth, Edward and Richard Plantagenet, supposedly murdered by their wicked uncle, King Richard the Third, they were immediately pronounced as the lost Princes.

After inspection by the personal physician of King Charles, John Knight, who readily confirmed they were indeed the two Princes, Charles ordered that the bones be placed within a memorial urn and caused it to be erected close to the tomb of King Henry the Seventh in Westminster Abbey. There they remained until the year 1933 when the urn was opened for the bones to be removed and examined by Dr Tanner the Westminster Abbey Archivist and professor Wright of the Royal College of Surgeons who brought in a dental surgeon, Dr. George Northcroft. Along with the human remains were found some animal bones, general building rubble and three rusty nails.

These eminent doctors subsequently reported that the human bones were of two children, one aged between twelve and thirteen, the other between nine and eleven. As the bones were prepubescent the sex could not, at that time, be verified. They reported evidence of a possible family relationship and that the elder child has signs of disease of the jaw and a stain on his skull, which Wright somewhat arbitrarily declared to be a bloodstain, the result of suffocation. On this basis they declared the bones were indeed those of the two Princes Edward and Richard Plantagenet.

The bones were resealed in the urn and there they remain to this day. Westminster Abbey authorities and the Queen have categorically denied access for modern scientific analysis, notwithstanding the recent discovery of the forensically identified remains of King Richard the Third at Leicester. Modern science has been able not only to identify the Leicester bones as being those of the king, but also changes in his diet throughout his life.

There is, therefore, a good reason for the obstinacy of the Westminster Abbey authorities; they know perfectly well the bones are not of the two Princes and wish to spare themselves the embarrassment that a scientifically proven disclosure would bring upon the Abbey. We are dealing here with a UNESCO World Heritage Site with over one million visitors per annum. If it were to be discovered the bones were actually indeterminate Londoners of later date than 1483, the date of the supposed murders, then they would be faced with the ignominy of having a public monument to a hoax.

A personal conviction that King Richard murdered the two boys is not dependent on the presence of the bones in the Westminster Urn. Even if the ossuary was opened and tests proved that they are not the remains of fifteenth century Plantagenets, the controversy would still remain much as it is. The power of the medieval melodrama is not easily defeated.

While there have been acres of print produced regarding whether the Princes were murdered or not, clearly something was going on in the year 1674 that required the bones to be "found" and the story given a new lease of life. It is evident, from a more critical examination of all the evidence we have to date, that the bones are not the two Princes. This begs the question why someone in the year 1674 wanted to resurrect the myth of the supposed murders one hundred and ninety years earlier.

Bones were found in the Tower of London that deliberately mimicked the ages the two boys would have been then.

Obviously there was purpose behind it.

Note. Because they were illegitimate and therefore barred from the English throne, technically the two sons of Edward the Fourth were not entitled to a royal prefix, but as this is how they are popularly known within this particular story, to avoid confusion they are thus referred to as Princes throughout the text.

1 - The Restoration

Charles Stuart, the eldest son of defunct monarch Charles the First entered London at the end of May 1660 to enthusiastic acclaim. The rule of the Puritans was over and England could return to the days of festival and fun. Holidays, that before the rule of Cromwell had for centuries punctuated the otherwise hard lives of the people, were restored along with the king. The tyranny of the father was forgotten and that of the son yet to be realised. In fact, though the newly restored monarch would turn out to be every bit as despotic as his father had been, yet his personal profile would be massaged by his absolute control of what we today would term the media. Thus he has gone down in history having the epithet "The Merry Monarch" attached to his name.

He had taken well a lesson from his father. Charles the First had written a book, with the cooperation of several others, which was published after his execution and distributed throughout Europe. Titled: "The King's Image" it was a series of essays justifying Charles' conduct during his reign, especially the last few years of it. The book was reprinted many times and was a major instrument of Royalist propaganda during the Commonwealth in England. Another whose attitude to propaganda might have influenced the restored monarch was the man who had ruled England immediately before him, Oliver Cromwell. Having banned the former King's book, he too made sure that public declarations regarding his rule would always be in his favour and there were extreme penalties on anyone who said or caused to be published anything that dissented from Puritan doctrine and its religious or political interpretation. The poet John Milton, a confirmed republican, wrote a counter to Charles' book – "The Tenure of Kings and Magistrates." It set down the ideal that all men are born equal, that a king was not ordained by God but ruled by the will of the people; thus there was no bar to a king being deposed. It was the beginning of modern democracy and as all new ideas, it would take many years before becoming adopted. England accepted with some reservation the restoration of monarchy and eventually it would be Milton's principle of government by parliament that would triumph, while the monarch would become a treasured figurehead, subject to the same laws as the people. In 1660, however, the monarch, in spite of the lessons of the recent past, still considered his rule to be absolute.

Cromwell had not controlled England without support and there was much residual Puritanism throughout the land. The matter of successive rule had not been properly thought through during the Commonwealth and so, when Cromwell died the only natural process the people understood was to offer the job of Protector to his son and heir. The problem here was that though a monarch's heir was bred for the job from infancy, Richard Cromwell had been brought up on his father's manor and had no particular training or inclination for a job that promoted him to engage in monarchical rule. The only practical course open to the mind of seventeenth century Englishmen, not yet being schooled in the principles of a democracy where the people have a vote, was to recall the son of the man they had, some years earlier, forcibly removed from his throne and then executed.

Not everyone welcomed the restoration of Charles the Second and some feared the consequences that might be visited upon them at his return. There were those living yet who had been instrumental in bringing about the execution of his father. Some would turn their coats and become extreme monarchists to preserve their lives; others would trust to the mercy of the new monarch. Many of these in the next few months would have their hopes and expectations dashed. John Milton, high on the king's death list had his books burned publicly. After some time on the run, he was captured and imprisoned in fear of his life. It was only the intervention of his powerful and influential poetic Royalist friends that saved him.

None of this was yet realised as Charles' splendid entourage entered his capital through the specially built and overdressed triumphal arch, constructed hurriedly to welcome him. Politicians, churchmen, aldermen of the city, representatives of the law and court, the trade guilds; all were vying to outdo each other in manic dedication to his sacred majesty. Musicians composed music in his praise and poets declaimed line after line of sycophantic verse and but a few wondered at the vacuity of it all. The common citizens cheered themselves hoarse and their ladies pledged themselves to him body and soul. Rarely had London witnessed such an outpouring of affection especially for a king who had won no battles, conquered no foes or even had to fight for his crown. His reign was to set a new tone for monarchy in England. From now on any fighting would be done verbally and surreptitiously amongst courtiers, politicians and churchmen. A monarch might be brought to a battlefield to observe, but he would never again take a place in the vanguard of a fight. The last one to do that had been Richard the Third and look what happened to him.

The diarist John Evelyn was voluble in his praise and could not help but prostrate himself in a short epistle titled "A Panygyric for the Royal Party" of which here is a sample:

Miraculous reverse! O marvel greater than man's council! Who will believe that which his eyes do see what before a twenty years confusion had destroyed: behold a few months have restored: But the wonder does yet more astonish, that the grief was not so universal for having suffered under such a tyranny, as for having been for so long deprived of so excellent a Prince: No more then do we henceforth accuse our past miseries; all things are by your presence repaired, and so reflourish; as if they even rejoiced they had once been destroyed. So as not only a Diadem binds your sacred temples this day; but you have even crowned all your subjects too; so has your auspicious presence gilded all things; our Churches, Tribunals, Theatres, Palaces, lift up their heads again; the very fields do laugh and exalt.

That is probably quite enough from John Evelyn for modern stomachs, but there is something he mentions here which is pertinent to our present enquiry. He notes that various institutions, previously suppressed, are to blossom again and one of these is the theatre.

Elizabethan and Jacobean governments had understood the latent power of the stage through its potential for influencing public opinion. Though not going so far as to permanently close the playhouses of London, yet all plays were scrutinised by The Master of Revels, a kind of early censor, before being given licence to allow performance. The monarchs Elizabeth I and James I loved the theatre and the players themselves enjoyed some royal protection. High nobles, active at court and in parliament, had their own player groups and it was tempting for them as sponsors to get the actors to speak lines according to their particular political viewpoint. This is why it was considered prudent to control what was being performed.

An example of the danger the playhouses represented to a monarch is illustrated in an event that occurred in 1601 towards the end of Queen Elizabeth's reign. The Earl of Essex, Robert Devereaux, had hatched a plot to dethrone Elizabeth and take the crown to himself. His plan was to get the people of London to rise in his support and depose her. To condition them for revolt, he employed the Lord Chamberlain's Men, of whom William Shakespeare was chief dramatist, to put on Shakespeare's play King Richard the Second. This is a story of the deposition and subsequent murder of a monarch. Queen Elizabeth is said to have cried "Think ye not I am King Richard the Second?" when she heard of the plot. As it transpired, the people of London stayed inside their homes when Essex rode into town and the Earl was easily overcome and arrested. He was later decapitated for treason on Tower Hill. Shakespeare and the Lord Chamberlain's Men were brought in for questioning and as they could show they were duped and entirely innocent of what the earl's intention had been, were let off. Though the plot failed, we can see how great value was credited to the power of the public stage and its potential to influence opinion. The means for exploiting this power would soon be employed by the newly restored monarch.

Puritans hated the theatre. Apart from the potential for the dissemination of Royalist propaganda, it was a hotbed of iniquity, frivolity and licentiousness, which condemned it entirely in their eyes. Prostitutes plied their trade within and around the playhouses while entertainments such as bear baiting and cock fighting went on in a variety of establishments in the streets around. All public theatres were closed under Cromwell's rule and those attending an illegal play might find themselves in the public stocks, while the players would be imprisoned, or worse. For twenty years, actors, playwrights, producers had been without employment and the people deprived of a highly popular entertainment. Now the theatres would open again and those who worked in the medium were understandably amongst the most voluble in praising the restoration of King Charles the Second – at first.

Not only the theatre had potential for spreading propaganda: there was also the printed word. In the period before and during the Civil War it was common for those who wished to do so, to spread their ideas in the form of a printed pamphlet or broadsheet. Commonly it was clergy who had their favourite sermons printed and distributed among the population. Others saw the pamphlet as a method of spreading a political message. Political pamphlet printing had been considered to be work of low grade before the Civil War as many of those who engaged in it were ill educated. Most of the common population were either illiterate or had very limited reading skills and so political pamphlets often took the form of a dialogue that was specifically meant to be read out loud. Broadsheets would tend to be more political in tone and were, in fact, the beginnings of journalism.

At the Restoration of Charles the Second, however, the first thing the new monarch did was to get control of the country's printing presses. Later in the reign, pamphleteer Roger L'Estrange would be appointed Surveyor of Presses and by 1683 had the authority to grant licences. Those not subject to his licence were closed and unlicensed printing was declared illegal. Royalist pamphlets and broadsheets were printed and circulated. These were produced to a higher literary standard as hitherto because the court had an interest in promoting their regime and the writers were, as a consequence, well educated.

Poets, at first, were eager to ingratiate themselves with the King and those previously sympathetic to the republican ideal had some considerable work to do in convincing the new authority of their commitment to the monarch. John Milton kept his head down and produced his famous work Paradise Lost, the story of the creation and fall of mankind, which served to promote Christianity. He would steer well clear of any political writing. Milton had been Latin secretary to Cromwell's Council of State and served with his friend and fellow poet Andrew Marvell to whom he dictated part of his poem Paradise Lost. Milton became totally blind by 1654. At the Restoration Milton fled to the continent where his friends hid him. Eventually he was persuaded to return to England under the promise of amnesty for republicans given by the word of King Charles. He spent some time in prison but escaped a death sentence by the influence of his powerful friends, principally the ardent royalist William Davenant. Milton had spoken up for some of them during the Commonwealth and saved their lives, and so the favour was returned. In particular, he had spoken for Davenant, who had been facing a treason trial under Cromwell and was to become a leading theatrical manager at the beginning of the Restoration.

Poet Andrew Marvell was MP for Kingston-upon-Hull during the final years of the protectorate and managed to convince the new regime he had changed sides and was elected MP for Hull in the Cavalier Parliament. Though not a Puritan he was a convinced parliamentarian and wrote satirically and secretly against the Court party in parliament. His writings against the monarchy were published after his death, they being too critical of King Charles' court to be safely made public during his lifetime.

At the very beginning of his reign Charles the Second needed good publicity. The political manoeuvrings that led to his restoration did not have the approval of the whole country. At first he went to considerable lengths to ingratiate himself with the common masses while persecuting those he termed regicides. The Puritans had not been defeated militarily, though their strictures on popular entertainment were unpopular with most folk. Restoration was not just about reintroducing monarchy to what had been a republic, but the return of fun and laughter, too. Be that as it may, many held tenaciously to the Protestant religious principles of the Commonwealth. Charles was not slow to realise this, yet he did have a hidden agenda and he quickly saw how jocularity might obscure it until, that is, he had established himself securely on his throne.

His father, Charles the First had been an absolute monarch and the son was of the same mindset. He had agreed, as a condition of his return, not to pursue and prosecute those who had brought his father to trial and had him executed. It was allowed that the premier regicides might be brought to account, but the majority would be pardoned provided they pledged allegiance to his rule. There were fifty nine signatories to the Death Warrant of Charles the First. Few considered this as being much of a threat as a number of them, including Cromwell himself, were dead anyway. Charles, however, had other ideas, but in 1660 had to bide his time.

As he established himself he began to become confident enough to exact retribution and soon former "regicides," that is those who had a part in the trial and execution of his father were arrested, tried and condemned to a traitor's death – to be hanged, drawn and quartered in public spectacle at Tyburn. The king's revenge extended to those regicides already dead, notably Oliver Cromwell, John Bradshaw and Henry Ireton. These were dug out of their graves and exhibited at Tyburn before being ritually decapitated and their heads placed on spikes above the Banqueting House. Cromwell had a monument in Westminster Abbey, which was destroyed. The Abbey contained the mortal remains of a dozen or so prominent parliamentarians and all were disinterred and thrown into a common grave.

After he had caught and disposed of those he could find in England, Charles sent his agents to arrest and bring back for execution the few who had fled the country, and who wisely had not trusted his so-called amnesty. Not content with those names on his father's death warrant, he began to persecute those who had merely been in attendance. Edward Dendy was the sergeant-at-arms of the court during the King's trial, not a signatory to the death warrant. His arrest was nevertheless ordered and he fled to Switzerland where he died in 1674. Two prominent parliamentarians fled to America: William Goffe and Edward Whalley and were shielded by the Puritan Dutch settlement of New Amsterdam on Long Island. In the year 1664 Charles sent a fleet of warships along with four hundred soldiers with the aim of capturing them. There was also a sub-plot to eject the Dutch and establish British rule in the colony. The citizens of New Amsterdam moved the fugitives to the town of Hadley, located on the edge of Indian territory set in a wilderness. The people there were Puritans and welcomed the two men. They were never captured. In all, the King managed to have executed twenty regicides and those closely associated with them. Others were imprisoned, sent to the plantations of Barbados in virtual slavery or died in prison. Many more were deprived of their homes and wealth.

Two arch republicans managed to save themselves by dishonourably betraying their fellows and becoming their chief persecutors. They were Monck and Downing, the latter managing to obtain a knighthood and have a street in London named after him and the former a dukedom. Thus they were rewarded for their role in capturing and condemning to a traitor's death their former comrades. General George Monck, formerly one of Cromwell's chief and most ardent supporters became after the Lord Protector's death a most determined Royalist and promoter of Charles' restoration. Monck, though, began as a royalist. He was with the royalist army at Nantwich, Cheshire, in 1644. The town was under siege by the king's forces under lord Byron. General Fairfax, who was at Manchester with the rebel army marched to relieve the town and captured, among others, George Monck. After considering the way the Civil War was progressing, Monck threw in his lot with the parliamentarians and rose to become a leading Civil War general whom republicans considered to be on their side. When Richard Cromwell went off into exile, Monck was instrumental in replacing the officers of the army with his own men and largely dispersing the regiments so that they could not resist Charles when he returned from exile. It was Monck who led the newly restored monarch into London in 1660. In this he was considerably aided by men who had turned Royalist either for pecuniary reward or from fear of their own lives.

We might not think much of Monck's personal integrity, but at least he began as a royalist and was thus returning to his former alliance. Perhaps the most odious of turncoats was George Downing, later Sir George. He was born in Dublin though his Puritan family moved to New England when he was a child. Hearing of the Civil War against King Charles the First he took ship and came to England where he joined Cromwell's New Model Army. Thus he was a republican right from the start. He worked as a ruthless spymaster for Cromwell in the Netherlands where many royalist exiles lived. After Cromwell's death many men were considering their position. Downing decided his nefarious talents might benefit the exiled King and so began working secretly in his cause. Downing worked tirelessly to have his erstwhile colleagues and fellow republicans either murdered or kidnapped and brought back to face a mock trial before being hanged, drawn and quartered as traitors. A man despised by both sides, (Pepys described him as a "perfidious rogue") yet he saved himself and prospered by his ruthless dedication to the new regime. Today he is remembered for having a London street named after him, which now contains the main residence of England's premier politician and the Chancellor of the Exchequer. It is not known what the present-day incumbents of the houses at number ten and eleven think of the irony of having their address named for such a turncoat – most of us might consider it apposite!

After the euphoria that the first days of the restoration had provoked, and with the example of people as Monck and Downing, it became obvious that though some might find advantage in the new reign, many would be persecuted, deprived of their wealth, even their lives and their families condemned to destitution. While it might be argued that in some cases their wealth had been plundered from former royalists in the first place, still it hardly endeared those affected to the monarch.

Then there was the question of Charles' religious affiliation. Parliament had decreed that his restoration depended upon his acceptance of the Protestant faith and the Church of England. Charles, however, had been in exile for many years in Catholic France and had become sympathetic to that doctrine. In the second year after his restoration he married Catherine of Braganza, a Portuguese princess, and she was a practising Catholic. Moreover, the king's brother, James, who began by flirting with the idea of becoming Catholic, later converted to that doctrine. James' first wife was Anne Hyde, daughter of Edward Hyde, First Earl of Clarendon, by whom he had two children, Mary and Anne. After she died, James married Mary of Modena - Maria Beatrice Anna Margherita Isabella d'Este, daughter of the Italian Duke of Modena.

Mary in particular was considered to be uncompromising in her determination to restore England to Rome.

By the year 1674 the king had not produced a single male heir. His queen had delivered three stillborn children, but never a living one. The common people generally reviled the debauched nature of his court. Charles had sired illegitimate male children all over London to his catalogue of mistresses. While in exile he had a son delivered by Lucy Walter, his mistress. This boy, who was given the name James Scott, was born at Rotterdam in 1649 and acknowledged by Charles as his bastard. He later became the duke of Monmouth. Rumours that Charles had actually married the boy's mother, making him a legitimate heir, was another problem the king would have to face. Charles denied there was ever a marriage, but the nature of rumour is potent. He managed eventually to score seventeen bastards. As if this were not bad enough, everyone knew that when the king died, unless he had a viable male heir to succeed him, it would be his brother James who would become king, provoking a feared catholic revival. In this year, mistrust regarding the king's catholic queen, Catherine, though without foundation, would nevertheless lead eventually to calls for her impeachment on a charge of High Treason. This did not come about because Charles would not permit it, but it did his popularity among his people little good.

Almost as if he was deliberately flouting the concerns of his people, his mistress, Louise de Kerouaille was also a Catholic and a French spy to boot. She had replaced Barbara Villiers, (Lady Castlemaine) as Charles' principal mistress. He ran her more or less currently with the actress Nell Gwynne who famously was mistaken for Louise by the people of London as she rode in her closed carriage. They began to shout and threaten her passage until Nell leaned out of the carriage and shouted, "Good people, please be civil. I am the Protestant whore!" That turned the situation around for Nell Gwynne, who was an actress at Drury Lane Theatre, but did little to enhance the reputation of Louise de Kerouaille. Much later, on his deathbed, it would be these three women that the king would express concern for, having finally converted to the Catholic doctrine – his queen Catherine of Braganza, the actress Nell Gwynne and Louise de Kerouaille. Of these three, only Nell was a Protestant, having resisted Charles' attempts at persuading her to convert.

Bad luck had also brought about the Great Plague of 1665, which only came to an end due to the Great Fire of 1666 when much of the old City of London was consumed in the flames. Charles had also provoked war with the Dutch, which had gone badly. In the year following the Great Fire, a Dutch fleet had sailed up the Medway and destroyed the British fleet supposed to be safe at anchor at Chatham docks. Ignominiously for the English navy, the Dutch boarded and captured the fleet flagship, the Royal Charles. This was the very vessel that had brought Charles to England from exile. They towed it back to the Netherlands as a trophy where the ship's coat-of-arms can be seen on display to this day at the Rijksmuseum in Amsterdam. It was England's greatest naval defeat. The Dutch destroyed fifteen ships while the English scuttled others to block the river. The biggest ships, the Royal Oak, the Loyal London, a new ship, and the Royal James were burned. Afterwards, this misfortune, on top of the Catholic question and the scandals of his personal life meant King Charles and his government feared a backlash from the people of England who were becoming increasingly critical of his rule.

By the year 1674 then, we can see that Charles and his government had become highly unpopular and desperately needed to turn the mood of the people towards that which he had enjoyed at the beginning of his reign.

Charles' strategy at the beginning of his restoration had been to use the printed word and public performance in the restored theatres to promote his monarchy. Perhaps what had worked in the heady days of the early 1660's could work in 1674 too, if only there was a way in which he could revive his past stratagem? No doubt his ministers were thinking along the same lines when an opportunity for promoting the reign presented itself.

Building modifications at the Tower of London were taking place below a stairway to St John's Chapel in the White Tower. This provided an opportunity to proclaim it the very spot where popular legend placed the bodies of the two boy Princes, the sons of Edward the Fourth. What if their remains were discovered there and how could this be used to promote Charles at this low point of his reign? Yet how could the events of over one hundred and ninety years past be of any relevance to the politics of Restoration England? Since the days of King Richard the Third, five Tudor monarchs had come and gone, there had been a religious realignment during the Reformation, a Civil War and republic that had changed the political climate and here was a third Stuart monarch on the throne. The age of Shakespeare had come and gone and everything associated with the England of yore was now considered old and tired. Nothing of medieval England remained and unlike the Tudors, the Stuarts had no fear of residual Plantagenet blood.

After the *chance* discovery of ancient bones, it merely required a suggestion they were the remains of the two Princes, Edward and Richard, thus reminding people as to how they were reputed, in popular story, to have met their fate at the hands of their tyrannical uncle, King Richard the Third. Here was an opportunity to further denigrate a monarch with a dramatic reputation for tyranny conveniently portrayed as such in the theatres. In drama, the tyrant was replaced by a returning exile who would restore peace and happiness to the land. Help in this subterfuge was immediately to hand - the playhouses also had particular problems at this time. Mutual self-interest was so much more effective than merely purchasing accomplices.

Today we are reminded how powerful is the story of King Richard the Third after his bones were excavated in Leicester. In this case it had already been properly worked out where his remains were likely to be. It was a proper archaeological investigation, not a mere chance discovery. Modern analysis soon confirmed it was indeed the lost king and news of the discovery spread right around the world.

Imagine the effect upon people living in the seventeenth century who, ignoring the problems associated with a casual discovery of some bones of the appropriate ages to fulfil the requirements of a tale of murdered Princes, willingly believed it was them simply because the circumstances fitted the old story. As a diversion a good tale works every time and as in any war, and this was a propaganda war, the first casualty is truth.

2 – The Restored Theatre

Once Charles the Second was crowned he wasted no time in restoring some of the entertainments banned by the Puritans and in particular the playhouse. All the old theatre buildings had been closed and destroyed in the twenty years of the commonwealth and so new ones had to be built. There was little about the new theatre that mimicked that of Elizabeth and James I; indeed, Tudor and early Jacobean theatre itself was denigrated, being inappropriate to the new age, its plays and playwrights considered vulgar and its language old fashioned.

Though Charles, and his brother James both loved being entertained at court, the usefulness of the public theatre for propaganda was not lost on a monarch who needed to establish firmly his rule. In this he was enthusiastically aided by those who had been dispossessed of their living during the Cromwell era, the producers, players and playwrights of England. Conscious that here was a two-edged weapon, Charles made certain that only plays licensed for public performance would be allowed. The monarch had to be sure of a safe pair of hands when managing a theatre and the first he chose were those of Sir William Davenant, a poet, playwright and follower of Charles the First, who had been knighted by him in 1643.

During the Commonwealth Davenant was arrested and condemned to death. He escaped that sentence by the intervention of his republican friend John Milton, whom we have already learned was similarly saved by Davenant when he too was in danger of the same fate at the restoration of King Charles the Second. It seems that, in contrast to the rest of society, the fraternity between poets and playwrights was stronger than the flexible loyalties demanded by contemporary politics.

William Davenant was born at Oxford in 1606 where his father, John Davenant was the proprietor of The Crown Inn and Mayor of Oxford. John Davenant was a vintner and because of the unhealthy atmosphere, he and his wife Jane moved from their original home in the South Bank area in London, where the playhouses were located. The filthy conditions and disease there had robbed them of their first six children. It was claimed that William Davenant was the godson of William Shakespeare who often stayed at the Crown when travelling between Stratford and London. Davenant was said to have fancied he wrote with the spirit of Shakespeare and this led to the unfounded rumour that he was the Bard's illegitimate son. Nevertheless, he had a clear interest in all things literary, particularly the theatre.

He attended Oxford University but left without taking a degree and went into the service of the Duchess of Richmond. Living in London in 1630 he contracted syphilis and though he was treated for this it seriously disfigured his nose, which made him an object of cruel ribaldry by his enemies. Originally it was Ben Jonson who was designated Poet Laureate by his contemporaries and this title was passed to William Davenant when Jonson died. He came to the notice of Queen Henrietta Maria and thus of King Charles the First. In collaboration with Inigo Jones he wrote several court *masques*, one including a part for the king himself. In 1640, the last of these in the reign of Charles the First was written by Davenant.

In this year the king's son and heir, Charles, was ten years old and no doubt had some acquaintance with those who provided entertainments at his father's court. No wonder, then, when the theatres opened again at the Restoration of the son, Charles the Second, it was Davenant along with Thomas Killigrew who were granted warrants to form acting companies and allowed them to open their own theatres. Davenant opened the "Dukes" theatre while Killigrew ran "The King's Company" playing in a new theatre at Bridges Street, (later Drury Lane) near Covent Garden.

Thomas Killigrew was also a dedicated royalist. As a youth he had been a page to Charles the First, and it seems his education was formed mainly by the court and in the playhouse. He followed Prince Charles into exile after the execution of his father the king. Killigrew was a Catholic and while they were in exile was appointed young Charles' representative in Venice. Before the Civil War, Killigrew had already written several plays, mainly tragic-comedies at which he excelled. At the Restoration, Charles made him Groom of the Bedchamber and later Chamberlain to Queen Catherine. He was noted for his wit and Pepys considered him to be in the *"office of the king's fool and jester, with the power to mock and revile even the most prominent without penalty"* (Samuel Pepys diary, 13th February 1668).

Killigrew's rivals, Sir William Davenant's Duke's Company performed at Dorset Garden on the banks of the Thames near the outlet of the Fleet River. The duke whom the players were named for was, of course, James, Duke of York, the king's brother. Both Killigrew and Davenant were favourites of the monarch and his brother James; they were also rivals in the theatre. Killigrew was given control of The King's Company with license to perform the plays that had formerly been the property of The King's Men, the old acting company that performed plays by Shakespeare, Beaumont and Fletcher. The company initially performed at the old Red Bull Theatre then in 1663 moved to the new Theatre Royal at Drury Lane, though then it was known as the Theatre Royal on Bridges Street.

Where the old plays were revived, they were rewritten to transform them into something suitable for a more sophisticated crowd, which people of the age imagined themselves to be. This applied to Killigrew's company more than Davenant's seeing as he had inherited the rights to perform the old plays once owned by The King's Men, William Shakespeare's former player group. Killigrew, however, was seemingly a poor manager and he had many problems with his actors and even resorted to bribery to keep some of them. He had much influence with the king and in 1673 he became Master of the Revels, thus being the occupier of this office in 1674. This office had less power of censorship than in Tudor times; the Lord Chamberlain was the man responsible for ensuring that the material being performed in the playhouses met with the approval of the Court. However, Killigrew, who would report to the Lord Chamberlain, still had some control.

While there is no political link with the fifteenth century, there is a definite theatrical one – the play The Tragedy of King Richard the Third, by William Shakespeare. The Bard's dramatic creation of the most famous and despised of all villains, the iconic crookback who came into the world after lying in his mother's womb for two years, and with a complete set of teeth and a full head of hair was a gift to Caroline propagandists. Here was a ready made allegory where the twisted and cruel king could be made to represent the former Lord Protector Oliver Cromwell while the almost saintly Richmond, Henry Tudor, was the epitome of a benign king who had restored justice to the land. The play was useful propaganda and Charles the Second would make good use of it.

Shakespeare's play had been popular too with the earlier court of King Charles the First before the Civil War. At St. James Palace on the 16th of November, 1633 the Bard's Richard the Third was performed before the King and Queen Henrietta Maria. The Master of Revels at that date, Sir Henry Herbert, records it in his office book. He tells us it was the first play seen by Her Majesty since the delivery of her son the Duke of York. After this, the closing of the theatres during the Civil War and subsequent interregnum, discouraged theatrical performances at Court.

Other works commenting on the early Tudor period were also being written at the time and it is apparent that even back in the reign of Charles the First the suspicion that there was something wrong with the alleged accusation of murder against King Richard the Third is documented. John Ford published a play in 1634: "Perkin Warbeck" where the eponymous hero claims to be the duke of York, thought by some to be the younger of the two boys supposedly murdered by King Richard. It was not performed then, nor indeed would it be until after the interregnum, but it was published so that people could read it.

Perkin Warbeck is a history play generally ranked as one of Ford's three masterpieces, along with his typically restoration theatre titles 'Tis Pity She's a Whore" and "The Broken Heart." T. S. Eliot went so far as to call Perkin Warbeck "unquestionably Ford's highest achievement. One of the very best historical plays outside of the works of Shakespeare in the whole of Elizabethan and Jacobean drama." Ford's primary historical sources for the play were: The True and Wonderful History of Perkin Warbeck by Thomas Gainsford (1618), and The History of the Reign of King Henry the Seventh by Francis Bacon (1622). In his play, Ford treats Warbeck with sympathy and compassion, though without actively promoting him as the lost prince, rather he strives for a neutral treatment, in contrast with the overwhelmingly negative tone of official Tudor versions of the story.

A manuscript of the play exists, though it is a late product, dating to around 1745, and offers little additional insight into the play. That hardly matters because it shows that the traditional story of the two Princes being murdered then buried in the Tower of London was not universally believed, and certainly any educated person in 1674 with an interest in history and the theatre must have known that. What we are dealing with, then, is not an investigation into the facts of the supposed murders but merely a publicity stunt where a good story trumps intellectual debate.

We can show conclusively that the royalist propagandists early in the reign of King Charles the Second deliberately used the theatre, and in particular the story of the murdered Princes, to promote their cause. It was convenient to present Shakespeare's villainous King Richard the Third as a metaphor for despotism (Oliver Cromwell) while comparing the noble and kingly virtues of Richmond, (King Henry VII) with

Charles' noble rule. Three years after the Restoration of the king, there was a play specially written to do just this. It was not Shakespeare's version but simply used his characterisation and creation of villainy, one already firmly set into the minds of the common mass, to suit the purpose of Caroline propaganda. The text of the play is lost but the prologue survives and this tells us all we need to know of its dramatic tone.

The prologue from the 1663 production.

This day we Act a Tyrant, ere you go
I fear that to your cost you'll find it so.
What early hast you have made to pass a Fine,
To purchase Fetters, how you croud to joyne
With an Usurper, be advised by me
Ne'er serve usurpers, Fix to Loyalty.
Tyrants (like children bubbles in the air)
Puft up with pride, still vanish in despair.
But lawful monarchs are preserved by Heaven,
And 'tis from thence that their commissions given.
Though giddy Fortune, for a time may frown,
And seem to eclipse the lustre of a crown.
Yet a King can with one majestic ray,
Disperse those clouds and make a glorious day.
This blessed truth we to our joy hath found,
Since our great master happily was Crowned.
So from the rage of Richard's tyranny,
Richmond himself will come and set you free.

The purpose of this play is clear. Charles and his followers knew perfectly well the power of the theatre to promote ideas that influenced public opinion and in the early years of his reign it seems to have worked. If we are to prove a link between the discovery of the Tower bones and Charles' theatrical propaganda machine, we need to find something current in 1674, the year they were "found."

The second theatre now advertised as being at Drury Lane opened in March that very year. The new theatre had been built by raising funds from subscribers who would obtain a return on their capital investment from the profits of the new theatre. The first theatre on the site had burned down two years previously, depriving the actors and managers their of income while the Duke's Theatre at Dorset garden continued to earn revenue. The Theatre Royal or King's Theatre had been a popular venue and so it was decided to rebuild it. Obviously, if the investors were to recoup their money it was imperative that audiences were enticed back to the new venue.

Thomas Killigrew, or rather his son Charles, had the license from King Charles to perform the old pre-restoration plays, one of which was Shakespeare's Richard the Third. The Theatre Royal at Drury Lane has a long affinity with this play. It was a theatre manager and actor Colley Cibber who undertook the first rewriting of Shakespeare's version of the play in the year 1700. Even later, another actor manager at Drury Lane, the famous David Garrick specialised and made famous the role of the villainous king. There is a painting of Garrick in the role of King Richard in the National Gallery, London.

It is thus tempting to think the business with the bones in the Tower had something to do with a publicity stunt involving

Drury Lane, but although the possibility cannot be ruled out, it is unlikely to be that simple. The first performance at Drury Lane in March 1674 was "The Beggar's Bush" by John Webster. The play list for that year does not reveal a performance of Shakespeare's Richard the Third. Tantalisingly, there is a gap in the record of performances, both at Drury Lane and at Dorset Garden of the plays performed in the months including July 16-17, when the bones were "found."

The problem is that Shakespeare's iconic villain is so entrenched in the common psyche that it is difficult to get beyond the Bard's version, but when we do, a whole new vista opens up before us. Shakespeare's creation was so potent that others in the restoration period began to plunder the original and use the conveniently created monster for their own purposes. This is what had happened with the 1663 production illustrated above – it was not the only one. It seems that, in looking merely for Shakespeare's Richard the Third we are missing the other versions copied by lesser playwrights for their own purposes, and during the Restoration period, that had certain possibilities.

In the year 1667, John Caryl published a play titled "The English Princess, or the Death of King Richard the Third." As already explained, this was a bad year for Charles due to the ignominy caused by the Battle of the Medway and the burning of English ships supposedly safely moored up the Thames at Chatham. Caryl's play is pure propaganda, performed not at Drury Lane, but the Duke's Theatre at Dorset Garden. Pepys records in his diary his attendance at a performance there and the King saw it too. The Princess in the title of the play is Elizabeth of York, the future queen of Henry the Seventh. In the play she has to fend off the unwelcome and amorous advances of King Richard who has a dishonest interest in her. Richmond (Henry VII) is the hero of this story and we soon learn he is cast for King Charles the Second while King Richard is the tyrannical Oliver Cromwell. Though its first performance was in 1667, the play was performed regularly afterwards and reprinted for sale in 1672 and again, pertinently, in 1674. This shows us that interest in the story of King Richard the Third and the murdered Princes was not only popular in that year, but was still being used blatantly for propaganda purposes.

The prologue of the 1663 play shown above survives because it was printed separately, presumably for advertisement, in a Covent Garden Gazette of the time. There were many plays specifically written to promote the Court Party by destroying the reputation of Oliver Cromwell and the republic. A typical one was Edward Howard's *The Usurper* performed in 1664, where he excuses the spiteful exhumation and mutilation of Cromwell's body, claiming one death was not enough for the usurper. Later Restoration playwrights considered themselves the epitome of wit and the plain storytelling necessary for propaganda, where the message must not be obscured by intellectual pretension, held no charms for them. John Caryl's work, however, is complete and it gives us an excellent insight as to how the story of Richard the Third was useful to, and was used by, the Court Party.

Caryl does not limit himself to illustrating the King's villainy, but comments on other contemporary personages. George Monck, the man who turned from monarchy to republicanism and then again to monarchy and prosecuted both ideals vigorously is given the character of Lord Thomas Stanley, another traitor who turned from and betrayed his lawful king, Richard the Third, to embrace the government of Henry the Seventh. Early in the play Lord Stanley meets with King Richard and informs him that Richmond is weak and his forces starving and in despair. The king is keen to have the powerful lord on his side.

King Richard:

My Lord, this service to the full does show
How much a King might to his subject owe:
For Richmond these, and these had Richmond prop't,
Had not your hand this budding treason crop't,
And now, my lord, I hope your forces are
Advancing hither, for I ill can spare
About my person, and within my call
Such troops as yours, and such a General.

Lord Stanley:

You are my sovereign (Sir) a double way
Your wisdom and your power bear equal sway,
But Sir, I fear the effect if we should join
And all our strength within one camp confine.

Here Lord Stanley is swearing true allegiance to King Richard but already is manipulating things to suit himself, so that he might change sides if necessary. King Richard is unsure of Lord Stanley and turns to Catesby for advice.

King Richard:

Unhappy fate of Monarchs that we must
Often depend on those we most distrust.
But of this Loyal Rhetoric (pray) how much
In your opinion will endure the touch?

Catesby:

Sir, I believe 'tis in his power to be
Your greatest friend, or your worst enemie:
The softness of his words makes but that found
With which all hollow bottoms most abound;
But his late actions I confess have gained
My faith to think his honesty not feigned.
The rising borderers by him supprest,
That he is found at heart give ample test.

Catesby is referring here to Lord Stanley's loyal action in the wars with Scotland in the latter part of the reign of King Edward the Fourth. He joined then with Richard duke of Gloucester (later Richard III) to defeat the Scots and return the town of Berwick to England. The allusion is obvious: here is a general who fought first on one side, then turned traitor in support of another. George Monck turned and became one of Oliver Cromwell's premier Generals yet he was the man who turned again to escort King Charles into London in 1660 and used the army to persecute his erstwhile republican friends and comrades. Caryl is thus placing a warning to the present monarch regarding the conduct of such men.

The play, though, is intended to promote the Court Party of Charles the Second and Caryl, to blacken the character of

Richard the Third reminds his audiences of the murder of the two Princes:

Catesby:

Miles Forrest is his name; a fellow stout
And yet so dull he never felt a doubt
Nor questions deeds ill relished by the laws:
He weighs reward, but measures not the cause.
Twas he, Sir, who out-went your swift commands,
When the two brothers fell by his bold hands.

Towards the end of the play, Caryl reminds his audience of the reign of the king's father and the tyranny of the subsequent Commonwealth.

Prior

But after this a Tempest does succeed,
Which Hell shall with contentious vapours feed;
This tempest will produce a deed so black, (the execution of Charles I)
That murder then shall an example lack.
But from this dark eclipse a Prince will rise, (Charles II)
Who shall all virtues of your race comprise.
Foreign and native foes (republicans) he shall o'ercome,
With force abroad, with leniency at home.

In 1674, should anyone attending The English Princess happen to miss the point, Caryl reminds them of its moralistic purpose in his Epilogue, which directly addresses Charles the Second.

Richard is dead; and now begins your Reign:
Let not the Tyrant live in you again.
For though one Tyrant be a nation's curse,
Yet Commonwealths of Tyrants are much worse:
Their name is Legion, and a Rump (you know)
In cruelty all Richards does outgo.

The message could hardly be clearer. Caryl alludes to the New Testament story of the Gadarene Swine, (Mark 5:1-13) where Jesus encounters a man possessed of a demon. He calls to the demon to give its name, which reply comes back: "Legion, for we are many." Fearing expulsion from the land, the demons ask to be transferred into a herd of pigs. This Jesus does, and afterwards they rush into the Sea of Galilee and are drowned. The allusion is that England had become possessed of the demon Republic, which King Charles had exorcised. The Rump in the epilogue refers to the remnant of the Long Parliament, (Rump) which was the one that abolished the House of Lords and the Monarchy and declared England a Commonwealth. It was dismissed by Cromwell in 1653 but it sat again in 1659. Monck secured the recall of its purged members in 1660 when afterwards it was finally dissolved.

In "The English Princess" John Caryl avoids Shakespeare's graphic description of a "poisonous bunch-backed toad" and seems content with a straightforward portrait of tyranny, which no doubt suited his purpose. It was not until the year 1700 that Colley Cibber would rewrite Shakespeare's version of the play and not only restore the twisted caricature, but enhance it. Cibber's purpose, though, was to provide entertainment merely and by that time we might think that the propaganda aspects of the character were extinct. That could not be further from the truth. Still today there are modern interpretations of Shakespeare's Richard the Third where the tyrannical aspect of the character is used to illustrate modern despotism. In September 2012 a production of the play was put on at The Old Globe in London where director Lindsay Posner used it to reflect on how modern dictatorships function.

Ian McKellen's portrayal on stage and film, set in the 1930's, shows us Richard as a Fascist dictator.

Kevin Spacey, during his time at The Old Vic put on the play and is quoted as stating that modern dictators base their ideas of kingship on English Monarchy!

A few more examples are given in Appendix 1.

By the year 1674 many were recalling the moral tone of Cromwell's government and comparing it favourably against the debauchery of Charles' court. Cruel executions of regicides during the first few years of Charles' reign were brought to an end, not necessarily because the king thought enough was enough, although this is what he pretended; the regicides had made brave and unrepentant declarations of republican principles from the scaffold and this began to have some influence with the mob. The fear that some in the country would think it preferable that the Commonwealth be restored was an ever-present danger for the Court Party. Thus the temptation to remind the people of the tyrant Cromwell as opposed to the reign of good King Charles, as portrayed in the theatrical propaganda of the early 1660's would become an imperative. As Charles' reign went on, things turned sour and perhaps someone of the king's party, observing the building work in the Tower of London remembered the traditional tale that the two Princes had been buried at some spot beneath a stair. It happened that there was a stair where the excavations for new foundations were being dug. It would have been easy to think some use might be made of it.

What if some human bones were "found" and these remains happened to be of two children of the right ages to correspond to those of the two Princes supposedly buried there? It hardly concerned the Court that it was simply a fictional tale and one that had no veracity. Educated courtiers might realise that, but they were hardly going to upset things by contesting with the king. In the common mind, the Tower of London was where the Princes were buried below a stair somewhere in the precincts and that was what mattered.

Whoever dreamed up the scheme must have had connections with the theatre world. As it happened, the King's Theatre Royal at Drury lane having burned down two years previously, was rebuilt to reopen in March 1674. Just four months later the bones of the Princes were "discovered." In the interim the other principal theatre in London, the Duke's Theatre at Dorset Garden had gained from the demolition of the Theatre Royal with almost exclusive performances. For Thomas Killigrew and his son Charles, who was now in charge of the new theatre, it would have been imperative to do everything possible to get audiences back into the King's Theatre. The discovery of the bones of the "murdered" Princes would reawaken interest in the iconic play King Richard the Third and the brand new King's Theatre Royal now advertised as being located at Drury Lane with Killigrew as Master of Revels was well placed to deliver it – or something similar. As for the Duke's theatre, they would naturally want to hang on to the audiences they had gained after the King's Theatre had burned two years earlier.

Here we have three interested parties who might be only too willing to propagate a publicity stunt and who would recognise the possibility offered by the construction work in the Tower of London, conveniently being carried out on the fancied burial spot of two boy Princes cruelly murdered by their wicked uncle. The King's Party clearly had a motive in turning again to the previously useful propaganda involving the story of King Richard and the Princes in the Tower. The King's Theatre at Drury Lane needed to get its audiences back after a two-years period of enforced closure and the Duke's Theatre at Dorset Garden would naturally want to stop their audiences migrating to the new theatre at Drury Lane. The two theatres had serious Royal connections: Drury Lane with the king, and Dorset Garden with his brother James, Duke of York. All that was required to awaken interest in the old but still popular melodrama was the discovery, in or beside the Tower excavations, of an appropriate set of bones.

Someone working surreptitiously for one, or a combination of any of the above three could easily obtain some bones of the right ages and along with fragments of the wooden chest they were originally interred in, get them to the building site in the Tower, there to be found. A scrap of velvet to ensure identification of noble birth and the job was done.

3 – The Bones

To perpetrate the fraud, it would be necessary to acquire a pair of skeletons of the right age; after all, they would have to sustain examination by the king's physician, John Knight, who might not necessarily have been party to the fraud. If the bones were of children of the right ages to correspond to the fiction that they were the two Princes, then there would be no compulsion to involve the physician in the fraud. Indeed, John Knight's innocence in the matter would be a decided advantage, as he would volubly defend his analysis if it were ever to be questioned. While in the present day, obtaining human remains for a clandestine purpose might seem an impossible task, finding a suitable set of bones in the seventeenth century was simplicity itself, especially when those interested in procuring them were right at the top of society.

In the seventeenth century, and for centuries before, the graveyards of London were full, and finding room to bury the dead within the city was a severe problem. To compound the difficulty there were spasmodic outbreaks of plague, most notably the Great Plague of 1665-6. This had an impact on the conventional burial places in churchyards where plague-dead were buried in communal pits. Churchyards were soon overwhelmed and separate pits for the burial of plague victims were dug all over London. The Great Fire of London finally defeated the Plague in 1666, though it consumed many of the old buildings of the city along with the infestation. By the end, the plague pits would accommodate the remains of nearly twenty percent of the city's population, around 100,000 persons in two years.

King Charles took himself off to escape the pestilence, along with his court. Most noble families also moved out of the city leaving behind those with nowhere else to go. Author Daniel Defoe created a fictional character that elected voluntarily to remain in London during the whole period of the pestilence. This allowed him to provide posterity with a graphic description of the conditions that existed then. Defoe was just five years old at the time and would not have remembered any details himself, but in later years through his interest in early journalism, he had learned enough to provide us with a good idea of what it was like. He records the general location of some of the plague pits, for instance: *"The upper end of Hand Alley in Bishopsgate Street was then a green field, and was taken in particularly for Bishopgate parish, though many of the carts out of the City also brought their dead thither."*

And again: *"A piece of ground beyond Goswell Street, near Mount Mill. Abundance were buried promiscuously from the parishes of Aldersgate, Clerkenwell and even out of the city. Thousands of bodies are thought to lie here."*

The locations of the plague pits from this time are mostly unknown now because few records were taken at the time, though many pits have since been unearthed during excavations for new building work in the city.

Other than plague pits, burials in London, indeed in most places in the country, were rarely deeper than two feet, sometimes three. At first the dead were buried as they always had been in shallow graves. We can see how shallow they were when we examine contemporary illustrations of the early plague pits. If ever there were an incentive to bury diseased bodies somewhat deeper, we might expect plague pits to be dug so, and in London this is just what happened. Again Daniel Defoe, through his fictional character of a saddler, informs us that in the churchyard of the parish church at Aldgate they dug a great pit: "*A terrible pit it was, and I could not resist my curiosity to go and see it. As near as I may judge, it was about forty feet in length, and about fifteen or sixteen feet broad, and at the time I first looked at it, about nine feet deep; but it was said they dug it near twenty feet deep afterwards in one part of it, till they could go no deeper for the water; for they had, it seems, dug several large pits before this. For though the plague was long a-coming to our parish, yet, when it did come, there was no parish in or about London where it raged with such violence as in the two parishes of Aldgate and Whitechappel.*"

Finally the magistrates who had charge of the regulations regarding plague burials woke up to the problem of shallow graves: "*They could not put more in one pit due to the order of the magistrates confining them to leave no bodies within six feet of the surface.*"

In the case of death from natural or other causes in a conventional graveyard, it was still the usual practice to bury the dead in shallow graves, and nobody thought it necessary to dig further down. This provoked certain problems, not the least with smell. It was not unknown for graves to be dug up by animals and the bodies dragged out to be gnawed at by stray dogs or rooting pigs. However, plague bodies excepted, in normal circumstances once a body had decomposed, the grave was opened up and the bones deposited in a charnel house, letting the grave accommodate a new occupant. In London, a period of twenty-five years was allowed. This was a generous term if Shakespeare's assessment was anything to go by:

Hamlet – How long will a man lie I' the earth ere he rot?
Clown – Faith, if he be not rotten before he die, as we have many pocky marked corses now-a-days that will scarce hold the laying in, he will last you some eight year or nine year. A tanner will last you nine year.
Hamlet – Why he more than another?
Clown – Why, sir, his hide is so tanned with his trade that he will keep out water a great while, and your water is a sure decayer of your whoreson dead body.

The origin of the charnel house is found in ancient Greek burial practice. Greece is a land where generally the ground is stony with little depth to the soil. Where the soil is abundant it tends to be reserved for agriculture and so the areas set aside for burial are few and inadequate for long-term interment. In Greece, a body was left in the ground to decompose for around two years before being disinterred and the bones placed in a charnel house. There was nothing disrespectful in this; it was considered that the bones represented the mortal remains of a person, not the flesh, which contained the soul, a residue of which persisted while there was flesh present. Thus once all flesh had gone there was no bar to removing the bones from a grave. In Christian practice a charnel house (*ossuarium* in Latin) is consecrated and therefore sanctified.

Habitually erected to face east, the bones of the people in it may safely await the Last Judgement.

The Westminster Abbey urn is, in fact, correctly termed an ossuary though this word was also used to refer to a charnel house. During the interminable warfare throughout history, particularly in medieval times, it was common for the body of a nobleman who died away from his home to be defleshed, a process known as calcination, and the bones returned to the land from where the deceased originated for proper interment. This would be accomplished by butchery, to remove the flesh, then afterwards boiling to strip the bones of any remaining tissue. Often the equipment for doing this would accompany the nobleman on his adventures. King Henry the Fifth had a cauldron in his baggage at Agincourt that would have been used for calcination of his body should he have been killed in battle.

There was a good deal of *skulduggery* involved in the practicalities of managing a graveyard. A sexton was in charge of interments and where a grave was disturbed it was his responsibility to retrieve any exposed bones and place them in the charnel house. Overcrowded graveyards led to human remains being exhumed deliberately early to make room for a new arrival, for which the sexton would be paid. In practice, the only persons to actually enter a charnel house were the sexton, churchwarden and the priest of the associated church.

Charnel houses were found in many places in England and interestingly there was one attached to Holy Trinity Church, Stratford upon Avon, close to Shakespeare's place of interment. The "bone house" dated from the fifteenth century seems to have been still in use during the Bard's lifetime.

46

There is a reference to such a place in his play Romeo and Juliet.

O, bid me leap, rather than marry Paris,
From off the battlements of yonder tower;
Or walk in thievish ways; or bid me lurk
Where serpents are; chain me with roaring bears;
Or shut me nightly in a charnel-house,
O'er-cover'd quite with dead men's rattling bones,
With reeky shanks and yellow chapless skulls.

Romeo & Juliet Act 4, Scene 1

Shakespeare, however, chose and paid to be interred in the chancel of the church, avoiding the charnel house altogether. An annex to the main church, the building was said to have contained a vault with "the largest assemblage of human bones" according to one Samuel Ireland, writing in 1795. At this time the charnel house was in a state of decay and in the year 1800 the churchwardens petitioned for its demolition. This was done and the basement filled with earth with the bones still inside the vault, where they remain to this day.

As recently as 1999 a charnel house was discovered in London. Originally it was attached to the graveyard of the priory of St. Mary, Spital. The charnel house was in use from the 14th to the 16th centuries and served as a consecrated depository for bones disinterred from the hospital graveyard to make room for more bodies. It was shut down at the Dissolution of the Monasteries on the order of King Henry the Eighth. The chapel remained above the charnel vault, which had been emptied and filled with earth until, in the year 1700 it was demolished. An office block stands on the site today but the vault has been preserved and provided with a viewing gallery.

Only two ossuaries remain in England with their collection of bones complete. One is at St. Leonard's, Hythe in Kent and the other at Rothwell, Northants. The Church of the Holy Trinity at Rothwell dates from the 13th century. In the year 1700 a sexton was digging close to the south wall to make a grave when the earth collapsed and he fell through to land upon heaps of human bones. He had inadvertently found an ossuary, or charnel house, that had remained forgotten and undiscovered since the Dissolution. The ossuary at Rothwell seems to have escaped destruction at the Reformation as the windows were obscured by earth at the outside of the building.

The Rothwell ossuary is a semi subterranean crypt that contains the skeletal remains of over 1500 people. Before the Reformation, bone crypts and charnel houses were common but at the Dissolution, most were either destroyed or converted to other uses, often a dwelling for the living. The common charnel house was usually a two- story building with a chapel above and a bone crypt bellow. Often they were attached to a church, as at Holy Trinity, but many stood as single buildings within or close to a graveyard. Typically, the crypt would be partially above ground with windows so that people could look down inside to view the mortal remains of their ancestors.

Charnel houses began to be constructed in Christendom after 1254 when Pope Innocent IV officially recognised the existence of Purgatory. This was a place invented originally to describe a kind of staging post between Heaven and Hell. A soul would taste of the pains of Hell depending on how many sins had been committed during life. Every one was a sinner, of course, and some would be allocated an eternal place in the nether regions with the rest of the damned. Most souls, though, having spent some time in Purgatory might eventually expect to enter Heaven depending on the number of masses said for them by clergy. Rich people might build a chantry chapel inside a church and leave money to pay for one or more chantry priests to say masses for their souls. Charnel houses built within a church, or if external with a chapel over, would contain the bones of poor people. There a single chaplain might say prayers for their collective souls. In this way the Church had everyone covered. After the Reformation the Roman Catholic practices were abolished and although deposition of bones in a charnel house still occurred, it did so mainly to free up space in established graveyards rather than secure mortal remains pending the last trump.

The Lady Chapel of King Henry the Seventh, where the Princes' ossuary is located is an example of an edifice built by a king in fear of his immortal soul. He spent an enormous amount hoping to secure safe passage for his soul through Purgatory and into heaven. Of course, Henry had a good deal of sin to expunge and he spent on his chapel accordingly for the times, the colossal sum of £14,000. At first the chapel had been intended as a shrine for King Henry the Sixth, who Henry Tudor tried to have canonized. This failed to materialise and when Elizabeth of York died in childbirth in 1503 she was interred there. Henry the Seventh followed her on the 21st April 1509 and soon after his mother, Margaret Beaufort. What was on view there in 1674 was not original. The chapel was despoiled and stripped of some of its fittings during the Reformation. Further depredations took place under Oliver Cromwell. The upper part of the fine screen around the tomb, most of the gilded images of the saints that adorned it, much of the stained glass of the Chapel and the original altars were all destroyed.

The ossuary containing the supposed bones of the two Princes was designed by Sir Christopher Wren and placed in the Lady Chapel in 1678. It has a Latin inscription that translates thus:

'Here lie interred the remains of Edward V King of England, and Richard, Duke of York, whose long desired and much sought after bones, after above an hundred and ninety years, were found by most certain tokens, deep interred under the rubbish of the stairs that led up to the Chapel of the White Tower, on the 17th of July in the year of our Lord 1674. Charles the Second, a most merciful prince, having compassion upon their hard fortune, performed the funeral rites of these most unhappy princes among the tombs of their ancestors, anno domini 1678.

Notably, the collection of bones at Rothwell contains animal bones mixed in with the human remains. This was no doubt due to careless exhumation but the presence of animal bones in the Westminster Urn might be explained in the same way, though it is unlikely they were brought to the Tower of London from a charnel house. It would be impossible to extract two complete skeletons from the casually heaped bones in such a depository. They must have been disinterred from a graveyard where there might well have been animal bones carelessly discarded and swept up with the human ones.

The thing that rules out the procurement of the bones from a charnel house is that not all the remains of a dead person were transferred there. Preference seems to have been to preserve the skull and thighbones, the rest being of lesser spiritual worth. This being so there would be few ribs or smaller bones of hands and feet; more complete skeletons could only have come from a conventional grave.

This preference for skull and thigh has led to speculation upon the common symbol for death or danger, the skull and crossbones popularly attributed to the flag of pirates. The Jolly Roger is mostly a fiction – pirates flew a black flag though it is possible one or two might have added the dreaded emblem. There are many medieval graves, and later ones, with this symbol engraved upon them. Today it is an icon for poison or something equally deadly and is immediately recognised as such by everyone. There is no shortage of theories as to the history of the skull and crossbones but none of them are proven. Its origins are shrouded in mystery. So far as the Catholic Church is concerned, God does not need a complete set of bones in order to reassemble the deceased on the Last Day. Perhaps this is why an ossuary is limited to collecting the major bones. Indeed, no mortal remains are required by God at all, seeing as many saints and martyrs were consumed to ashes in the fire and thus have no mortal remains to reassemble.

As is apparent by the date on the monument, the Westminster bones were stored for nearly four years before deposition in their marble ossuary and nobody knows where they actually were during that period. The skeletons were far from complete when examined in 1933 but this does not mean they were in that condition in 1674. Souvenir hunting might be a reason for the loss of some bones and we have no way of knowing if the original bones were replaced to disguise such theft. Perhaps this explains the presence of animal bones, though it is unlikely someone stealing a souvenir femur would replace it with a chicken leg!

Restoration London after 1666 could almost be said to be a necropolis occupied both by the living and the dead. Familiarity with death, always close due to disease, casual violence and public executions was after this year exacerbated by the experience of the Great Plague. Afterwards, the living had become used to dealing with heaps of dead bodies and were not as sensitive when handling corpses as we are today. Judicially, the period was probably as brutal as any in English history. Those caught and convicted of treason by their association with the former Cromwellian regime were ritually butchered in public, being hanged and taken down alive, their genitals cut off and burned then their entrails pulled out of their living bodies. Next their heads were struck off and their bodies cut into quarters to be displayed at various points in the city. Heads were boiled then covered in tar for preservation and mounted in prominent spaces. In 1661, the head of Oliver Cromwell, whose body had been taken from his grave in Westminster Abbey and ritually hanged, was set upon the roof of the Banqueting House along with two other prominent republicans that were similarly dealt with, Henry Ireton and John Bradshaw. When Cromwell was taken from his tomb in Westminster Abbey it is reported that the stench was overpowering, yet it did not deter the public spectacle of his body being hanged.

Other dreadful sights could be seen all over England. The sentence for piracy was to be hanged on the seashore at the low tide mark so that the incoming tide would submerge the bodies, which were then attacked by all manner of marine life. Highwaymen would be hanged at a crossroads, then encased in an iron cage and left to rot. Their bones would eventually drop through to the ground below their cages.

In a century where rotting corpses were deliberately displayed prominently in public by order of the government, it would be no problem whatsoever to find someone of hardened sensibilities who, for a small consideration, might procure the right kind of bones for a certain purpose and say nothing of it. As we have seen, there were plenty of sites where suitable bones might be obtained. Disposing of corpses had become casual and disrespectful, particularly among those who had dealt with plague victims. Someone who was paid to acquire a set of bones to order would not be particular as to what other debris might be collected with them.

After their examination by Charles' physician, John Knight, the whole lot, including any debris that was taken up at the time of the *discovery*, seems to have been stored away for four years, then unceremoniously dumped in the marble urn. Clearly this was not the respectful interment we might expect for royal bones. What was missing is any trace of the wooden coffin or the scrap of velvet cloth placed there to denote that the bones belonged to the high nobility.

4 – A Likely Story

Who were the Princes in the Tower? They were the two sons of King Edward the Fourth named Edward and Richard with Edward being the eldest. Their father died somewhat suddenly in 1483 and it was then revealed that his marriage to his queen, Elizabeth Wydville had been bigamous, as he had already been contracted in marriage to another, one Eleanor Butler. This rendered all his children of his second marriage to Elizabeth illegitimate and thus barred from royal succession. King Edward had two brothers who were thus next in line to the throne. George duke of Clarence would normally have become king at this point but he was dead, having been under attainder due to his conviction for treason in 1476 and executed by order of King Edward his brother. Clarence had one son and a daughter who were also barred by their father's attainder and the boy was living in the north of England under the protection of Richard, duke of Gloucester. This left Edward's younger brother, Gloucester, as the only qualifying prince of royal blood and so he became King Richard the Third.

The royal brothers Edward the Fourth, George duke of Clarence and Richard of Gloucester (RIII) were of the House of York and they were opposed by another branch of the Plantagenet family, the House of Lancaster. These two branches had been in violent contention over right to the throne for years in the period now known popularly as The Wars of the Roses. In 1483, the year of the supposed murders of the two sons of Edward the Fourth, Lancastrian supporters had no legitimate candidate to call on to challenge the Yorkist right to the throne, so they were forced to settle on a man of dubious claim through an illegitimate line that came down from the reign of Edward the Third (1327-1377) through a mistress of his third son John of Gaunt. His name was Henry Tudor and he was living in exile in Brittany styling himself the earl of Richmond.

Henry Tudor's grandfather had been even more obscure, being the paramour of the dowager queen of Henry the Fifth, Katherine de Valois. After her husband King Henry died she lived quietly and one Owen Tudor was a minor landowner and steward in her household. She had three sons by Tudor and one of these was Henry's father. There was no contract of marriage between Katherine de Valois and Henry Tudor; indeed this would have required the permission of the English Parliament, she being a dowager queen. Some have tried to manipulate history to pretend there was a marriage to try to firm up the Tudor claim, but the plain fact is there is no such record.

The whole of this period is shrouded in Tudor manipulation of the true facts and it began during the reign of King Richard the Third by the spreading of a rumour that the two Princes, Edward and Richard had been murdered by their uncle, who had usurped their throne. King Richard had moved the two boys into the Tower of London for their own safety. The elder boy, Edward was said to be sick and attended by a physician named John Argentine. There is no actual evidence for this, nor that he suffered from a disease of the jaw. As in everything to do with the murder story we are dependent almost entirely on fabricated Tudor propaganda. Having said that, it is of course possible he was sick; there were plenty of maladies in the fifteenth century that could carry a person off, the tender ministrations of a physician being high on the list.

The reason they needed protection was due to the Tudor claim. Being of dubious lineage Henry Tudor could not claim a right to the throne by blood, but should he marry a royal princess, then his progeny would have a true claim through her. None of the European royal houses would countenance a marriage to Tudor so his plan, hatched by his mother, Margaret Beaufort, was for him to marry the eldest daughter of King Edward the Fourth, Elizabeth of York, (The English Princess in Caryl's play) sister to the two Princes. The problem here was that she, along with her sisters and brothers, had been declared illegitimate by parliament. Should Henry become king, however, he could order parliament to overturn the material fact of her bastardy, thus providing him with a *bone fide* royal bride and eventually legitimate offspring. Of course, in overturning her bastardy he would also legitimise her brothers thus making the elder King Edward the Fifth with his brother Richard of York next in line.

For the Tudor plan to work, these two boys had to be dead. This was why they needed protection, not from their uncle King Richard the Third, but from the Lancastrian agents of Henry Tudor. While they lived, his and his mother's scheming was all in vain. In order to murder the two boys they had to be somewhere they could be got to and being in the Tower of London rendered that difficult. In fact, it is by no means certain they were in there at all. An earlier attempt at *rescuing* them was made by a Lancastrian mob, which failed. It was directly after this that the two boys disappeared. It is entirely possible King Richard got them out to a safer place.

Rumour of their murder was fabricated with the intent of forcing King Richard to display them publicly, thus revealing where they were. This he naturally refused to do and then possibly things started to go wrong. If the elder boy, Edward had been sick when he entered the Tower, it is reasonable to think he might have died there of his affliction. Nobody knows what happened, but if this was the case then the surviving boy was in even greater danger from the Tudor faction, it being easier to isolate and kill one boy rather than two. Moreover the rumour of their murder, albeit false, was already public so Prince Richard's death would automatically be laid at the door of King Richard. With Prince Edward already dead, what more proof could there be that he murdered both of them? The only way out would be to get the boy away to somewhere he could live in safe obscurity. His continuing survival after Henry Tudor became king was thus a source of extreme agitation to the Tudor by the ever-present possibility of his return. His was a better claim than Tudor's and thus he might seize his rightful place as King of England.

After the Battle of Bosworth, when by a combination of treason and bad luck King Richard was defeated and Henry Tudor became king, Henry did everything he could to get hold of the remaining princes. There were, in any case not two, but three princes – the two sons of Edward the Fourth and the son of his brother George duke of Clarence. This boy was the fifteen years old Earl of Warwick, also named Edward. Before the Battle of Bosworth this boy, the earl of Warwick, was being safely cared for by King Richard at Sheriff Hutton Castle in the north. Immediately after the battle, the fortunate Henry Tudor had him brought to London and placed in the Tower.

Warwick was in no immediate danger because Henry believed Richard of York was alive somewhere and finding him was Tudor's priority. All that was required to declare Edward of Warwick King of England, however, was to lift the attainder that had been placed on his father, a far easier task than overturning the material fact of illegitimacy that Henry was to order for the woman he made his queen, Elizabeth of York. This being so, this third prince would never leave the tower alive.

Henry Tudor's reign was to be plagued both by rebellion amongst his people, who were loath to accept him, and for his draconian rule. Matters were made worse by the occasional appearance of those claiming to be a Plantagenet prince. The imprisoned Earl of Warwick was considered too young to be a candidate at this time. Significantly, it was commonly the younger of the two sons of Edward the Fourth, Richard of York who was thought to be still alive. If such claims were fabricated, as Henry Tudor tried to make out, then it would make sense to promote the elder of the two Princes, Edward the Fifth, yet it almost always settles on Richard of York. This indicates that those of the English and European nobility, who were in a position to discover the truth regarding the disappearance of the two Princes, knew perfectly well the elder boy was dead and therefore it was futile to promote him. By the same logic, this presumes the second boy was alive and out there somewhere. Certainly by his behaviour Henry Tudor believed this, and the residue of Plantagenet claimants haunted his son, Henry the Eighth too. Both these Tudor monarchs were paranoid to the point of extreme anxiety bordering on insanity in this regard.

The most serious and tenacious claimant for Henry Tudor's throne of England came from the young man who emerged in the year 1491 and named rather derogatorily by King Henry as Perkin Warbeck. Modern historians now tend to declare Perkin a fraud, but there is a certain amount of factual manipulation involved and such opinion is by no means certain, given everyone must work with reference to the manic propaganda of the Tudors and dubious witness statements, some extracted under torture. What is certain is that Henry the Seventh spent a considerable amount of time and money trying to capture him. When he finally got hold of him after six years of trying he imprisoned him in the Tower right next to Edward of Warwick who was still a prisoner there. Now there were indeed two princes in the Tower with Edward of Warwick by blood the true king of England. Though Richard of York (Perkin) might have been tainted by the original charge of bastardy yet he still had a firmer claim than King Henry.

It was not long before there was an attempt at escape by these two, who had been allowed to communicate with each other. Both were easily recaptured, accused of treason and sentenced to death. They were hanged at Tyburn, Perkin having "confessed" to being an impostor. His face had been ruined so the crowd would not be able to detect the physical resemblance to his father, Edward the Fourth. Thus Henry the Seventh judicially murdered two young men, one without doubt by blood, the rightful King of England and the other probably a close second. By this time, though, the two were young adults.

Henry Tudor did claim one piece of evidence that the two sons of King Edward the Fourth were murdered back in 1483.

It was an alleged confession by Sir James Tyrrell, demonised later by Shakespeare, as indeed was King Richard. The confession was never produced and is mere hearsay, yet Sir James under torture is said to have admitted he had been instrumental in having them murdered.

No matter what differing accounts of the period tell us, we can see from all this that the eventual fate of the two boys Edward and Richard cannot be declared with anything approaching certainty. Tyrrell's confession was never produced and in any case was extracted under torture, or the threat of it. He was executed immediately afterwards. The one man who absolutely needed the boys to die was Henry Tudor and if they were still in the Tower of London after the battle of Bosworth that would certainly have been their fate. However, they would have been two years older by then and the elder a young man. As such their bones would identify their true ages. The likelihood is that the two boys died at separate times and in different circumstances. What is certain is that whomever the bones in the Westminster Abbey urn belong to, they are not the sons of Edward the Fourth.

* * *

It is important to realise that the discovery of the bones of 1674 was not the first time at the Tower of London when the *Princes* had been declared found. After Shakespeare's invention of the iconic villain Richard the Third, it was merely necessary to turn up a bone fragment for someone to declare the Princes were discovered. Earlier, for instance, in 1603 a sealed room in the Tower was opened where two figures were discovered seated at a table. The remains disintegrated upon discovery and the room resealed. These, though too young, were nevertheless said to be the bodies of the two Princes. At another time a skeleton was discovered inside a sealed room at the top of a tower. This was at first declared to be a royal prince, but subsequently discovered to be that of an ape, presumably escaped from the menagerie, which had climbed up and unable to get down again, starved to death. There had been a menagerie at the Tower since the reign of King John, the first record being 1210 and it was only shut down in 1832 when the Royal animals were sent to Regents Park Zoo. In 1670, King Charles gifted a lion from the menagerie to the King of Denmark.

What all this demonstrates is that there is a section of society poised and all too ready to proclaim any bone uncovered in the Tower of London as one of two Princes. It is in this atmosphere that the bones of 1674 were pronounced as being them, thus confounding any attempt at proper investigative analysis.

Though the location of the bones of 1674 was at an arbitrary spot that tradition suggests the Princes were buried, it is just that: tradition. Indeed, a proper reading of the traditional tale confounds it. The man who set down the story, Thomas More, gives us the only opinion on the location of the burial site in his book "The History of King Richard the Third" stating that the boys were murdered and buried below a staircase under a heap of stones. Thomas More was brought up in the household of bishop John Morton, who was a rabid Lancastrian and supporter of Henry the Seventh. More was promoted under the next king, Henry the Eighth and rose to become Chancellor until he fell foul of Henry's wishes regarding his divorce from Katherine of Aragon. We might ask, then, that if the burial site was known to King Henry the Seventh why didn't HE have them dug up and thus prove they were murdered and buried there. It would have saved him all that trouble with Perkin Warbeck who many believed was the younger of the two princes, Richard of York.

The obvious answer is that he knew they were not there. Someone, however, might helpfully excavate at a later age and to get around this considerable problem, Thomas More fabricated a get-out story. More informs us that the Princes were removed from the spot under the stairs shortly after the supposed murder by an unidentified priest and taken away to a secret place for burial. This eliminated the problem of any excavation failing to unearth the Princes and future-proofed the fabulous tale of murder by their wicked uncle. This part of More's history was ignored in 1674 but mentioned in 1933 by William Wright in his report, who promptly discounted it! If More was truthful regarding the murder of the boys and their place of burial, then logically he was truthful about the later removal of their bodies also.

After that the wretches perceived, first by the struggling with the pains of death, and after lying still, to be thoroughly dead: they laid their bodies naked out upon the bed, and fetched Sir James to see them. Which, upon the sight of them, caused those murderers to bury them at the stair foot, meetly deep in the ground, under a great heap of stones.
Then rode Sir James in great haste to King Richard, and showed him all the manner of the murder, who give him great

thanks and, as some say, there made him a knight. But he
allowed not, as I have heard, the burying in so vile a corner,
saying he would have them buried in a better place, because
they were a King's sons. Lo the honourable courage of a King!
 Whereupon they say that a priest of Sir Robert Brackenbury
took the bodies again, and secretly entered them in such a
place, as by the occasion of his death, which only knew it,
could never since come to light. Very truth is it and well
known, that at such times Sir James Tyrrell was in the Tower,
for treason committed against the most famous prince King
Henry the Seventh, both Dighton and he were examined, and
confessed the murder in manner above written, but whither the
bodies were removed they could nothing tell.

More's is the only account that claims to tell us the Princes
were buried in the Tower of London, but not where. He merely
states it was at the foot of some unidentified stairs. He does not
tell us which stairs. Nowhere is it said or suggested that the
location by the White Tower was the designated spot. This is
useful for the prosecution of a subterfuge because it means
bones found in any hole in any part of the Tower with a stair
close by may be designated the Princes' gravesite. In fact, this
is exactly what happened in 1674. There is no factual evidence
to support the story. Another problem is that the murders were
supposed to have taken place within the Garden Tower (today
known as the Bloody Tower and described thus by Dr Tanner
in his part of the report). To support the story we must believe
that the bodies were placed into a chest or coffin, carried
through the busy Tower precincts, then deposited in a suitable
excavation ten feet below the stair at an entrance to St John's

Chapel, where there was bound to be some human traffic, all without anyone noticing!

Tower of London – The route the murderer's would need to have taken

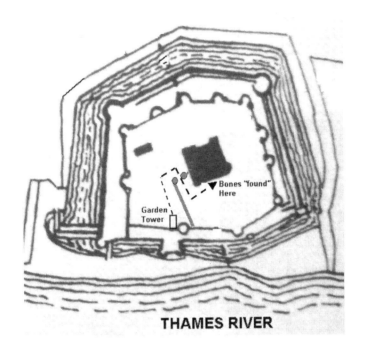

So whose were the bones found in 1674? Clearly they cannot be the Princes if, as More writes, they were disinterred by a friendly priest and removed, and if he was making the whole thing up, then there would be no bodies there to discover in the first place. Either way the spot below the stairway, whichever it was, must have been empty after the time of the supposed murders. That being so it would still have been vacant in 1674. As for the mother of the two Princes - Elizabeth Wydville certainly knew something of the truth. She never admitted that her boys were dead to the frustration of her son-in-law, King Henry. Fearful of what she knew, he shut her up in a convent at Bermondsey where she died in 1492.

The story that More reports is based on the version related by Polydore Virgil that Sir James *Tyrrell* had confessed to the murder of the two Princes. Shakespeare, in his play "The Life and Death of King Richard the Third" accuses *Tyrrell* of arranging the murders but again, we are dealing here with drama, not reality. Sir James had been a staunch supporter of King Richard, but after Bosworth managed at first to come to an accommodation with Henry Tudor. His Yorkist sympathies eventually got the better of him and he was executed in 1502 for his involvement in one of the many Yorkist plots to depose Henry. Before then he had been Captain of Guisnes Castle near Calais, part of the English Pale in France. Henry had caused the castle to be besieged in order to prise out a reluctant Sir James who had taken refuge there. He finally managed to do so with a promise of amnesty, which Henry, true to character, promptly reneged on. Tyrrell was arrested and subsequently confessed under torture to the murders of the boys but was unable to say when the deed was done, where they were buried or what manner of death they suffered. The *confession* was never produced and modern historians suspect it was merely a rumour put about by King Henry after the executions of Perkin Warbeck (aka Richard of York) and the earl of Warwick to discourage the idea there might be yet another Plantagenet Prince somewhere in the shadows.

We can see that the murder by Tyrrell's henchmen on the order of King Richard the Third, and clandestine burial of the two Princes, is a fiction invented to provide political obfuscation. Other problems with the discovery of the bones are soon identified. The most pertinent is the depth at which the bones were said to have been found: ten feet down through stone foundations within the Tower of London. The fact that they were in a spot tradition, if not the full story, might have placed them should alert our suspicions. We are invited to believe that the murderers of the two Princes excavated to a depth that, in 1674, took a team of workmen several days to achieve. Medieval burials, indeed most burials until Victorian times, were shallower than today yet these were supposed to have been discovered ten feet down within stone foundations! People in London at the time the bones were *discovered* were not interested in the archaeology; indeed there was no such science. What they had presented to them was an exciting story of murder by a man they readily identified as a monster, the villainous King Richard the Third. We are dealing here with what was demonstrated as a *chance* discovery, not an archaeological exploration as the recent Leicester dig, which actually discovered the bones of King Richard where there was good evidence they might be found under what was a car park.

Here is an original report on the finding of the Tower bones.

> *"Upon Friday the 16th day of July, 1674 in order*
> *to the rebuilding of the several Offices in the*
> *Tower, and to clear the White Tower of all*
> *contiguous buildings, digging down the stairs*
> *which led from the King's lodgings, to the*
> *chapel in the said Tower, about ten foot in the*
> *ground were found the bones of two striplings in*
> *(as it seemed) a wooden chest, which upon the*
> *survey were found proportionable to ages of*
> *those two brothers viz. about thirteen and eleven*
> *years. The skull of one being entire, the other*
> *broken, as were indeed many of the other bones,*
> *also the chest, by the violence of the labourers,*
> *who cast the rubbish and them away together,*
> *wherefore they were caused to sift the rubbish*
> *and by that means preserved all the bones. The*
> *circumstances of the story being considered and*
> *the same often discoursed with Sir Thomas*
> *Chichley, Master of the Ordinance, by whose*
> *industry the new buildings were then in carrying*
> *on, and by whom the matter was reported to the*
> *King."*

Most accounts, including those written in 1674 ignore the
technical difficulty for the murderers in surreptitiously
excavating ground to a depth of ten feet. Astonishing when we
recognise this was supposed to have been the year 1483 in the

Tower of London, a royal palace and fortress crammed with people – servants, soldiers, cooks, armourers, courtiers, the Royal Treasury – it even had a menagerie. A ten foot excavation must, perforce have a great heap of spoil beside it corresponding to the depth of the hole. To prevent it collapsing in on the diggers it would need to be shored with planking and ladders provided to let whoever was digging there climb out. Seeing as the two boys were supposed to have been murdered and the crime concealed by a *secret* burial, commissioning a team of workmen as murderers seems an odd way of going about it. After the burial a great mound of earth and stone above the grave would either have had to be levelled or some of it transported away.

The sensible explanation is that by the time the hoaxers had conceived the idea, found a suitable pair of skeletons then smuggled them into the building site, the excavations had reached that particular depth. Had the scheme been conceived sooner, or prosecuted faster, no doubt the remains would have been *found* at a shallower level.

Another problem that should alert us to the idea of a hoax of some sort is the fact that the bones are of differential ages to correspond with the ages of the Princes when they were supposed to have been murdered. Of course they were. What are the odds that not one but two skeletons of these respective ages might be uncovered? It is conceivable that skeletal remains might be found there, or anywhere in the castle precincts. This was not unusual at the Tower and had occurred several times already and habitually pronounced as being the Princes. The suspicious circumstances in this case, though, stretch the possibility of coincidence too far.

King Charles the Second appointed his own personal physician John Knight, to examine them and his opinion was confirmed in 1933 when the bones were last examined. We can be sure that the bones are of the right relevant ages to correspond with the murder story, but that does not confirm their true identities. Whatever was going on in 1674 was very sophisticated and involved the monarch, or it was understood that the monarch would become involved.

It has been suggested that because archaeological excavations often reveal constructions from a former age as being several feet below the current ground, that this somehow accounts for the excessive depth of the skeletal finds of 1674. However, the site is at the foot of a staircase giving access to a door and spiral staircase. That door was still there in 1674 and the level of the ground the same as it had been one hundred and ninety years previously. Ancient sites that are several feet below ground are at depth because they have been subsequently built over. The Tower of London too stands on ground that had a Roman fort upon it hundreds of years before. Human remains from this period have been unearthed regularly during new constructions that are penetrating a superimposed layer. The moat around the Tower still reveals the occasional bone or two, so the finding of human remains there is not unusual. For this to apply to the place at the Tower in 1674 where the burials were allegedly found, the ground before the door must have had some sort of new construction imposed on it since 1483. This was clearly not the case as the same door was still there in 1674 and being used for access to the chapel above.

Fortunately, we now have clear evidence as to the depth that a medieval burial might be found in similar circumstances. As a king, Richard the Third was buried not in secret, but at the command of King Henry the Seventh below the entrance to the choir of the Church at the Greyfriars Abbey in Leicester, a place of great sanctity reserved for the highborn. We might think, therefore, there would be no impediment to providing Richard with at least a decent plain chest. Felons executed at Tyburn were granted that. So far as it can be determined there were no signs of funerary vestments or accoutrements. The grave was shallow, of course, between two and three feet in line with medieval practice, and hurriedly dug; it was too small to accommodate fully his body and the king was simply dumped in there. No time was spent digging a hole big enough to contain a sarcophagus, or even a modest chest, yet there was no particular urgency, seeing as this was not a clandestine burial.

At the Dissolution of the Monasteries, the building at Leicester was destroyed, thus any bodies interred there might be expected to lie deeper than the medieval normal two or three feet. The site, thereafter, became a house and garden, and later still a car park, yet King Richard's remains were discovered close to their original depth and nowhere near the ten feet suggested for the Princes' interment. For the Princes to have been found ten feet down in a chest in the Tower of London, we are asked to believe the secret murderers actually went to this extra trouble. Some have seriously suggested the Princes' remains could have migrated to a depth of ten feet after 190 years, while King Richard's remains were still at their original depth over 500 years later. The idea is ludicrous of course, but it is strong testimony, once more, to the power of story, which ignores inconvenient observation.

The Westminster bones were found along with what was claimed to be a wooden chest, or coffin. There was also a scrap of velvet – an expensive fabric that only royalty and the highest nobility would wear. This conveniently informs a casual examiner that the associated bones were of high caste. Of course this scrap of velvet was soon lost and we have no way of examining it. There was no sign of it in 1933, nor of the wood of the coffin. Today we would determine the relative ages of these artefacts to ensure they all correspond to the same time period. The velvet may have been placed there and probably was, simply to indicate royalty. That even a scrap of velvet could have survived for one hundred and ninety years after a hurried interment is unlikely in the extreme.

* * *

Let us turn, then, to the inspection of 1933. The report that was subsequently delivered is seriously problematic. It appears, when reading the reports of the eminent men who conducted it, Lawrence Tanner, the Abbey archivist, and Professor William Wright, President of the Anatomical Society of Great Britain assisted by Dr George Northcroft, then president of the Dental Association, that they had already made up their minds they were looking at the remains of the two Princes. The very title of the report gives the game away: *Recent Investigations regarding the Fate of the Princes in the Tower*. We might think this title was the innocent product of the conclusion to the report, but nevertheless, it suggests there is something of sensationalism about it.

Tanner, as the Westminster Abbey Archivist certainly had a vested interest in "proving" the bones were of the Princes. His part of the report was a potted history of the story of King Richard's short reign and the traditional tale of murder. William Wright seems to have been satisfied with Tanner's version of the historical story and analysed the remains accordingly. To be fair, however, Lawrence Tanner writing later in 1969 and being the only one then living who had actually seen the bones and handled them, explained a problem with the wording of the report.

It will be noted that Professor Wright for convenience assumed that the bones were those of Edward and Richard. This was, perhaps, unfortunate for it has led some people to suppose that we definitely identified the bones with those of the Princes. No such claim was made, and I was, in fact, particularly careful in the Paper which we read before the Society of Antiquaries to make no such identification, and to adopt a cautious and "not proven" attitude throughout.

It is true that Dr Tanner, in his final words in the conclusion to the report did not actually state emphatically that the bones were of the two Princes, but he did heavily suggest it by his use of semantics:

It follows that if these bones are really those of the princes, and Professor Wright concludes that not only is there nothing from a scientific point of view against it, but that the evidence

72

is "definitely more conclusive than could, considering everything, have reasonably been expected", then we can say with confidence that by no possibility could either, or both, have been still alive on the 22nd August 1485, the date of Henry VII's accession.

Other existing authorities commented on the details in the report and some pointed out that one of the skeletons might be female and though there was the ability to determine sex in 1933, (something lacking in 1674) yet there had been no attempt to do so. The teeth, which were unerupted, indicated the possibility of one of them being female. It was also established that the age gap between the two sets of bones was less than the three years that separated the two princes Edward and Richard. Wright stated that Wormian bones (islands of bone) of unusual size and similar shape on both crania were evidence of consanguinity, while the lachrymal bone, smallest and most fragile of the face of one of the boys was abnormal. Dr. Northcroft, after an examination of the teeth to determine age, was in agreement with Wright's findings. Both sides of the lower jaw of the elder child, *presumed* to be Edward the Fifth, exhibited extensive evidence of the bone disease osteomyelitis, a condition that in medieval times was incurable.

Wright pointed to a stain on the jaw of one and thought that this might be a bloodstain consistent with suffocation. Sir Thomas More had stated in his book that the Princes were smothered with pillows in their beds by Sir James *Tyrrell*, John Dighton and Miles Forest. As we know, *Tyrrell*'s supposed confession is non-existent, dubious and merely part of the fiction. Here we can detect the triumph of story over intellect.

73

Clearly Wright was affected by the dramatic tale he had probably learned at school and simply interpreted what he was seeing accordingly. Why else would he attribute the stain to suffocation when he could not possibly know even if it were blood? In any case blood would have been suffused in soft tissue, not bone. He took scrapings of the bone where the stain was and had it tested. Though he reports in a footnote the result was inconclusive, yet Wright still insisted in his main text that there was no doubt it was blood.

A Remarkable feature of Edward's facial skeleton was an extensive stain reaching from just below the orbits to the angles of the lower jaw. The stain was of a distinctly blood-red colour, of a dirty brown colour below, and was obviously, as shown by the gradual fading away of its margins, of fluid origin. I have no doubt it was a blood stain. Its presence, together with the complete separation of the facial skeleton, lends support to the traditional account of the manner of the brother's death – suffocated "under feather bed and pillows, kept down by force hard unto their mouths."

Footnote: I endeavoured to obtain corroborative evidence of its nature by scraping the parts but failed to obtain more than a little powdered bone which, subjected to spectroscopic examination, gave no results.

Nowhere in his text does Wright refer to the possibility that such a stain might have been the result of proximity to the rusty nails found with the remains, yet his description of the stain might just as easily be attributed to it. Everyone concerned with the opening of the urn comments on the nails. After the first brief mention of these objects, there is nothing more said about them, which, with regard to the above, seems somewhat remiss. Nails would have been pure iron at that period and when it rusts, iron has a distinct red colour which, when placed close to another object will stain it. The colour of such a stain is exactly as Dr. Wright describes in his report. Nowhere do we find a suggestion that this should be accounted for in the examination of the bones. Indeed, there were other commentators on this supposed bloodstain made after the report was published in 1935 and they do not pick up on it either. We find an account of it in Dr. Tanner's recollections of 1969.

Mr. P. M Kendall, the distinguished biographer of King Richard the Third had submitted the anatomical dental evidence in the Tanner and Wright report for independent expert comment. These were:

Dr. W.M. Krogman, Professor of Physical Anthropology in the Graduate School of Medicine of the University of Pennsylvania, Dr Arthur Lewis, Orthodontist of Dayton, Ohio, Professor Bertram S.Kraus of the Department of Anthropology, the University of Arizona, and to the English doctor, Dr. Richard Lyne-Pirkis of Godalming, Surrey.

They were of the opinion (a) that it was not possible to determine the sex of either child (b) that the stain on the jawbone was not a bloodstain resulting from the suffusion of suffocation, and (c) that the precise ages of the children, as estimated by Professor Wright and Dr. Northcroft, were open to doubt although they agreed in spite of this, if the bones were

really those of the Princes, both children were still young
enough to have met their death as historically stated i.e. August
1483.

Next is the problem with the scraps of wood found with the
human remains? We are asked to believe that the murderers
were the first in history, and probably the only ones ever, to go
to the trouble of procuring a wooden coffin for their victims,
then excavating a secret hole in difficult ground big enough to
receive it. This idea is, of course, preposterous, but makes
perfect sense if the human remains had been disinterred from a
London graveyard and brought to the Tower building site to be
dumped on the debris of the excavation. In that case they
certainly would have originally been buried within a wooden
chest. It also means that the bones would probably have been in
the ground for a considerably shorter period than the 190 years
that is claimed. Professor Wright actually and unconsciously
suggests this view in 1933 in his report thus:

While as a general rule the bones were dry and of a light
brown colour, being largely, if not entirely devoid of organic
matter, the single metacarpal bone and to a less degree the two
phalanges of the fingers were exceptional in being of an ivory
white colour, suggesting that a certain amount of organic
matter was still present. Such a difference may be attributable
to the three bones in question having been in some way
protected from the more complete desiccation, which the other
bones had undergone. If, as I conjecture, the two bodies lay
face to face with the hands folded between them, the conditions

76

necessary for the more perfect preservation of the three bones may have been present.

The survival of any organic matter on bones buried for 190 years is a suggestion dubious in the extreme, but it might be possible for bones more recently interred, more so if they had been buried within a wooden chest in a London graveyard.

The bones, however, in 1933 were by then supposed to be 450 years old and still showing signs of organic material being present!

This being so, there must have been rather more of this evidence present in 1674, which was presumably ignored by John Knight. There followed four years in the air before interment in the Westminster Urn so the likelihood is that the bones were much less than the declared age otherwise, given the circumstances of their history, after 450 years there would be no organic material to identify at all. Note in this supposed scientific report that in order to explain this anomaly Wright freely confesses to *conjecture* in trying to make the story fit the observable evidence.

His conjecture is based on the idea that the bones of the elder child, whom Wright insists on naming as Edward the Fifth, must have been laid on his back with the younger, whom he names Richard, facing him on top. This is supposed to have suppressed complete breakdown of organic tissue between them. His reason for this conjecture is that the bones of the elder child are more complete and better preserved than the younger. This, he speculates, is due to the workmen breaking into the middle top of the wooden chest and damaging the upper skeleton, the lower one being protected by the upper.

Having a fixed belief that the two children originated from the Tower excavation, it would not have occurred to him that it is more likely the missing bones were lost when transporting them from whichever London graveyard they had actually come from. Those who dug them up were just as likely to damage the remains as the workmen at the Tower might have done, then leave some behind in the original grave. Moreover, if workmen at the Tower had actually broken into a wooden chest containing human remains, they would hardly have ignored the fact and simply dumped them and continued with their work. Their own natural curiosity would have prompted them to report their find.

Had the bones been from the Tower excavation then the chances of there being two complete skeletons is high. If they had been dug from a remote graveyard and transported secretly to the Tower site, then the chances that some would be lost in transit is high. Thus we can conclude the latter is the greater probability.

Any assumption that the bones of 1674 are the remains of the Princes is entirely dependent on their ages. Nobody as yet has been able to determine the actual year or years the Westminster remains come from. Modern scientific analysis would determine that very quickly, which is a good reason why the Westminster Abbey authorities will not grant permission for the urn to be reopened.

As noted above, Professor Wright, in his examination, commented that the two sets of remains were at different stages of preservation with the remains of the elder child in a better condition than the younger. This is curious and requires some thought. It is entirely reasonable to consider that if the bodies

78

were originally interred at different times, one of them, in this case the skeleton of the younger boy, being in the ground some time before the other, would naturally show greater signs of decomposition. This view is not contradicted by the material fact that there were fewer bones found of the younger child. The coffin of the elder child being dropped upon it during that child's later interment might explain damage to the body already in the grave.

It has the merit of being more probable than Wright's explanation where he supposed workmen clumsily damaged the remains and kept quiet about their find. Even if this were so, it would not reduce the number of bones present; merely alter their condition. Of course, if the younger actually did lie on top of the elder, then logically there would have been more bones present of the younger, seeing as these would be thrown up first. Conversely, being deeper in the ground and under another coffin in a graveyard would increase the likelihood of some bones of an earlier interment being left behind in the vacant grave. Here is Wright's statement from his Report:

"I imagine that when placed in the elm chest in which they were found, Edward lay at the bottom on his back with possibly a slight tilt to his left, that Richard lay above him face-to-face, and that when the chest was discovered in the seventeenth century, the workmen broke into it from above and near its middle. I am led to these conclusions from the fact that much more of Edward's skeleton was present than of Richard's, since presumably lying deeper it was less disturbed, and from the fact that the extreme upper and lower portions (viz. the head and feet) of Edward's skeleton are so well preserved."

Wright's conjecture, that the elder child lay deeper in the ground under the younger, would, if anything provoke a greater amount of decomposition, but he reports the opposite condition. We might reasonably expect both skeletons to display the same degree of preservation, if, that is, they died and were buried together at the same time. Of course, Wright was locked in to the idea the two *were* murdered and buried at the same time and hardly concerned himself with another possibility. It was enough for him that the differential in ages of the two skeletons was appropriate to what he expected to find; he gave scant thought as to their individual vintage. Had it not been for the fabulous story that infected intellectual control of the investigation, he might have looked further into this anomaly.

All this points to the bones having been in the ground rather less than 190 years when they were *found*. They were coffined and thus must have come from a common graveyard. The indicated presence of organic material and the identifiable remains of their coffin as being elm points clearly to this being the case. There is no actual evidence the bones were taken from the excavation – they were found in the building rubble discarded by the workmen. That they were actually buried at the impossible depth of ten feet was, and still is, assumed. There is no evidence whatsoever to show this was the case. Murderers do not provide coffins for their victims. If there had been one it would have been seriously decayed and yet the scraps of wood that were found with the bones were readily identified, without scientific analysis, not simply as wood, but specifically as elm. This too points to the material being in the ground for a much shorter period than was being claimed.

Once we realise the likely ages of the bones, we can easily clear up other confusing points in the Tanner and Wright report. Let us place ourselves in the mind of whomever it was procured the bones for the purpose of prosecuting the deceit. Given that there were powerful Court interests involved, there would be sufficient money and authority available to procure surreptitiously the requisite material.

All that was required would be to glance at the burial register of a graveyard to identify where bodies of the right ages were interred. This would almost certainly be the object of a double interment because it would have been so much easier to dig open one grave rather than two. If there were two children in a single grave then the chances are high that they were related.

The high death rate among juveniles in the seventeenth century would soon have provided the right coincidental material. It mattered little if the remains were male, female or one of each. All that mattered, for the purposes of the hoax, was that they were close to the respective ages the Princes had been at the time of the supposed murders. In this case, what would appear to anyone examining the remains in 1933 would be evidence of consanguinity, thus reinforcing the idea that here were the two Princes. Seeing as the children were in their grave, it is obvious they must have died of some disease or other, which should not surprise us. Evidence of this, too, might be apparent, and indeed it was on one of them. It was not necessary that the children died at the same time; they may not have come from the same grave either.

It was common practice in 1674 to disinter old bones and place them in a charnel house. There would be nothing unusual in this. For the hoax to work, mortal remains would have to be fully decomposed, meaning that the gravesite would be around twenty-five years old and ready for possible reuse. No priest, churchwarden or parish sexton would interfere with such work so long as they were presented with a satisfactory reason. If the remains really are related in blood, then this argues they came from a family grave, which would point to the original location being a churchyard rather than a hospital burial ground.

When we stand back and look at the actual evidence as it is presented to us, then the thought that the bones were of the fifteenth century recedes and only the power of a dramatic story sustains that belief. Tanner and Wright, nevertheless, strongly suggested the remains to be the Princes in the Tower and the bones were respectfully wrapped in lawn cloth then resealed in their urn where they remain to this day.

Modern visitors to Westminster Abbey, when standing before the marble ossuary, are probably paying homage to a pair of children from London's poor who are interred in a royal monument. Perhaps that should please us rather more than lamenting the deaths of two royal princes who, had they matured, could well have made decisions that would have provided England's graveyards with even more material.

There is another set of bones that we know for certain are from the fifteenth century. Anne Mowbray, duchess of York was the child-bride of the younger of the two sons of Edward the Fourth, Richard of York. The two married when she was just five years of age and he four and a half years. Anne was the only daughter of John Mowbray, duke of Norfolk and when he died she became heiress to great wealth. King Edward arranged, not quite legally, the marriage so he could get control of the Mowbray fortune for his son. King Edward, of course, would have management of it during Richard's minority. Dispensation from the Pope was arranged as the two children were first cousins and, therefore, too close in blood for a normal arrangement.

Anne died at the age of eight years and she was buried, sealed in a lead coffin at Westminster Abbey. When he became king, Richard the Third restored her fortune to her proper heirs, principally John Howard whom he also raised to become the duke of Norfolk. Strange conduct for the grasping tyrant Shakespeare and the Tudors would have us think him to be. Later still, Henry the Seventh, who was planning a chapel for himself at the Abbey had Anne's coffin moved into a vault below the place where her mother still resided, the Abbey of Minoresses, which was run by the nuns of Order of Poor Ladies. Over the years the location was lost and the Abbey demolished.

In the year 1964, workmen digging on the extinct site, broke into the lost vault there to discover her coffin. It seems those whose occupation is building demolition are somehow fated to be drawn to the old story. The object was taken to the London Museum. A plate on the coffin positively revealed exactly who she was and her date of death.

Here lies Anne, Duchess of York; daughter and heir of John, formerly Duke of Norfolk, Earl Marshal, Earl of Nottingham, Earl of Warenne, Marshal of England and Lord of Mowbray,

Seagrave and Gower; the late wife of Richard Duke of York, the second most illustrious Prince of Edward the Fourth, King of England, France and Lord of Ireland; who died at Greenwich on the 19th day of November in the year of our Lord 1481 and in the 21st year of the reign of the said Lord King.

On examination, after the lead was cut open, inside was the skeleton of a child wrapped in the remains of her burial clothes. The skull still had remnants of brown hair attached. Six months of study followed whereupon the remains were interred back in Westminster Abbey close to her original grave and the monument supposedly containing the bones of her husband and his brother.

Laurence Tanner, still there as Keeper of the Muniments and Librarian, was present when the coffin was opened and in his book "Recollections of a Westminster Antiquary" he informs us as to what he observed.

I saw the body a few days after the coffin had been opened, and a very distressing sight it was; and again after it had been cleaned and beautifully laid out as a skeleton in its lead coffin. She had masses of brown hair.

Dr Tanner goes on to describe the eventual reburial at the Abbey:

There on a summer evening, after having lain in state covered by the Abbey Pall in the Jerusalem Chamber, the body of the child Royal Duchess was laid to rest. It was a deeply moving and impressive little service conducted by the Dean in the presence of a representative of H.M. The Queen, Lord and Lady Mowbray, Seagrave and Stourton (representing Anne Mowbray's family), the Home Secretary, the Director of the London Museum and one or two others.

At least we can be certain there are two from that time who were lost, now found and properly interred: Anne Mowbray at Westminster Abbey and King Richard the Third in Leicester Cathedral. It is impossible to read Dr Tanner's account above and not think upon how the same dignity was accorded King Richard at his reburial. Perhaps providence has provided some sort of amends for the calumny that a distorted history has brought down upon King Richard's head?

5 - Shoehorn History

The whole business surrounding the fate of the sons of Edward the Fourth is dubious. It began with a fiction specifically designed to force King Richard the Third to reveal the whereabouts of the two boys. That fiction translated into Tudor propaganda and the story has been used as such ever since. Where the bones found in the reign of Charles the Second are concerned, rational minds might wonder that a story intended as reality might be rather better thought out.

Here we have the tale that two boys were murdered then buried in a coffin below a stair, which, by its very nature is a thoroughfare. The chosen place for concealment is the busiest Royal castle in England; the country's military and administrative centre no less. Rather than take the bodies away for secret disposal, the murderers' choose somewhere that people are bound to pass through constantly, day and night, seeing as the stairs gave access to a chapel where a daily round of prayers were said, beginning with the midnight office. The idea is preposterous and if it were not for the power of story would be laughed to scorn.

We have had presented to us, however, the description of a hump-backed villain, two years in his mother's womb and born with a full head of hair and a set of teeth. Uncle to the two boys, he despicably murdered them and usurped their throne. If it were not for this popular melodrama, devised and propagated by theatre, investigators might have questioned the legitimacy of the skeletal remains found in 1674 right from the start. Of course, the remains hardly needed to be positively identified.

It was enough that the bones corresponded to the ages of the boys at the time of their supposed deaths. The purpose of the story was, as it always had been from its inception in the days of Henry the Seventh, to desperately bolster by propaganda the reign of a monarch whose throne was in jeopardy. This was all very well in the seventeenth century when such a fabulous tale might have gained popular credence, which was, after all, the singular point of it. Four years later, as the story ran out of steam and when someone finally got around to it, the bones were placed in their marble monument there to provide Westminster Abbey with an entertainment.

There is less excuse for such naivety in the modern world, yet is seems the power of the story overrides reason and so the shoehorn comes out in an attempt to make the evidence fit no matter how much manipulation is required to do so. Investigators into the identity of the bones found in the Tower of London in 1674 insist on merely debating whether the remains belong to the boy princes or not. Those who conclude the matter is unproven and those who believe the bones are not the Princes stop at that point. Nobody seems to ask what should have been the very first and most obvious question: "If not the Princes, then who might have put the remains there, and why?" Once satisfied with whichever conclusion regarding the dramatic murder tale takes their fancy, investigators lose interest. If a modern enquiry were to be run along these lines, the investigators would be held to ridicule. The plain fact is that investigators have no interest other than speculating around a dubious medieval story of murder.

This very tendency should alert us to the probability that in 1674 there was some sort of hoax at work, which might be worth looking into. The business was simplicity itself. All that was required was to place in a spot, which was being conveniently excavated near a stairway, the skeletal remains of two children of the relevant ages corresponding to that of the Princes in 1483 and then stand back. The drama of the story did the rest of the work.

The impossible depth of ten feet, and the great distance from the supposed murder site, should have set alarm bells ringing; instead we find a great deal of ingenuity being exercised to "explain" how that might be feasible, when common sense dictates otherwise. Indeed, the whole business is nothing more than *shoehorn history*. We have seen how Tanner and Wright set out right from the start to investigate whether the bones were as stated on the inscription of the ossuary in Westminster Abbey. Their whole examination was tainted with a belief in the murder story, in spite of a good deal of contemporary evidence that at least one of the Princes survived Bosworth.

Nobody questions the fact that the remains had been coffined, something which secret murderers would not contemplate. Bloodstains are claimed to be present even after tests prove inconclusive and no attempt at pointing out that the rust from iron nails found with the remains might be the cause of it. There are strong clues to the bones being much nearer to 1674 than 1483 yet these are ignored. They do not fit the dictates of the story.

Now these things have been pointed out, no doubt someone will eagerly emerge willing to offer scientific evidence it is possible that organic material could remain on the bones 450 years after their history up, under and above ground, but all this would do is testify even more strongly to the power of story.

This certainly was the case in Tanner and Wright's report when it was speculated how the bodies were arranged in the coffin to account for it; something they could not possibly know or begin to prove.

The presence of coffin wood, claimed by Wright in his report as being elm, notwithstanding it was supposed to have been in the ground for 190 years in 1674, might be subjected to the same fanciful analysis, but that hardly accounts for the fact that the material was not scrutinised to determine its age at the time of its discovery and is now lost. Nobody in 1674 would have paid much attention to it. Identification as it being elm must have resulted from a casual observation, indicating a relatively short period underground, otherwise time would have obliterated so ready an identity.

It is tediously predictable that someone might claim, as these were supposed to be Royal Princes, that the murderers' would have procured a coffin and respectfully wrapped the bodies in velvet. Perhaps a priest from the chapel above the burial site might have been invited to say a few words over their bodies? Flippant this might be, but it is fair comment on the conduct of some investigators.

We do, though, have proven details of how a royal corpse might be disinterestedly disposed of. When the skeletal remains of King Richard the Third were discovered recently we find no sign of a coffin, or any kind of cloth material. The position of the body suggested there might have been a shroud, but no material evidence other than supposition. There was a nail, though, which speculators immediately pronounced as an arrowhead because it had become located near the spine. Subsequently, sober analysis showed it to be but a nail, probably of Roman origin, that had already been in the ground before the king's body was put in, and which through time had migrated there. Imagine if the original false identification had been left as an arrowhead with no further corroboration? Here is a recent example as to how speculation depends on story, which, if given credence leads us astray.

In the case of the discovery of the skeletal remains at Leicester, what did occur was a proper scientific analysis, carried out independently by the University of Leicester. There were no presuppositions so far as the team analysing the remains were concerned and anyone who had an interest in proving they were actually the remains of King Richard the Third, was kept out of the matter altogether. Contrast this investigation with that of Tanner and Wright. While it is understood forensic science permits a much better analysis of skeletal remains today, yet the above precautions were considered absolutely necessary to ensure there would be no assumptive contamination of the evidence. Modern investigators were all too aware as to how the power of story might corrupt an otherwise sound opinion. This was clearly not the case in 1933.

Of course, if someone placed the bones at the Tower of London to exploit the drama, we must ask the question: who would do it, and why? This small study has done just that and it is clear there is another story running alongside the fabulous fiction. From the very start of the reign of King Richard the Third, dubious politics have been engaged to use his story as a metaphor for political villainy. It began with the Tudor faction who needed to give the impression the two sons of Edward the Fourth were dead to free up the scheme to proclaim their sister,

Elizabeth of York as legitimate, without shooting Henry Tudor's ambiguous claim in the foot. King Charles the Second, at his restoration, had no qualms whatsoever in using the story as propaganda to promote his own Court faction. The idea that the troubled king repeated this strategy, or someone of the Court did in 1674 is an entirely reasonable argument. The same convenience has been made of the fictional story ever since.

There is a codicil to this hypothesis. Throughout the reign of Charles the Second we find the villainous character of Richard the Third in a variety of plays, not only Shakespeare's and many with a contemporary political bias. The character was also be used against the monarchy. In 1680, John Crowne adapted Shakespeare's Henry the Sixth, Part Two into an anti-catholic rant. It was sub-titled: the Misery of Civil War, performed at the Duke's Theatre (Dorset Garden) and printed in the same year. In this parody of Shakespeare's play the malign character of the duke of Gloucester (Richard III) is enhanced, his crookback is emphasised while he and his brothers' philandering in the play becomes a comment on King Charles' behaviour. John Crowne was known to have a moral repugnance for the Court. The political intent was deliberate as the *Exclusion Crisis* was in full cry in this year. (This was an attempt in Parliament to exclude the king's brother James, a Roman Catholic and heir presumptive, from ascending the English throne). The tables were turned as towards the end of his reign (Charles died in February 1685) the drama that once promoted his monarchy was being used to satirise and reflect badly upon it.

Those who condemn Richard the Third as an unrepentant villain should perhaps think carefully upon their own persona.

Many of us can claim some relationship with the fifteenth century monarch. It has been estimated that up to seventeen million people in the UK may be related in some way to the medieval king. Perhaps that is why we are drawn to his story. His character has something of so many of us, or someone we know, embedded within.

It would appear, then, that the soul and body of King Richard the Third remains in the common mind a convenient model for tyranny, one whose story may be used indiscriminately for immoral purposes.

His mortal remains rest at last in a proper tomb in Leicester Cathedral, yet there are those who insist on ascribing the foulest of crimes to him, merely for the sake of an entertainment. At least, though, we know the bones at Leicester are actually his, which is more than can be said of those in the marble urn at Westminster Abbey.

Appendix 1 - So Many Richards

The theatre has been manipulating the story of King Richard the Third for propaganda purposes from the day it was written to the present. Its usefulness as political metaphor looks set to continue well into the future. Here are a few examples from the twentieth century and into the twenty-first.

Laurence Olivier, directed by John Burrell at the Old Vic in 1944, was the principal in the production in this year. As with his Hamlet, it was reckoned to be a definitive performance. The production was taken around the world and then in 1955, Olivier himself directed the film version. It is a fairly straightforward portrayal with "interpolations" by Coley Cibber and David Garrick. It is intended as entertainment and does not attempt deliberately to comment on contemporary politics, though the subject matter might be interpreted as such in any age.

Barry Kyle directed an all-female production at the Globe, London in 2003. Kathryn Hunter took the part of King Richard. Here we have the drama being manipulated to make a Feminist point.

Jonathan Slinger's Richard in 2008 was played in modern dress and intended to represent the never-ending story of despotism and how it recreates throughout history. It illustrates George Santayana's famous adage: Those who ignore the lesson of the past are doomed to repeat it.

Colonel Gadaffi inspired Kevin Spacey's portrayal of King Richard in 2011. Costumes for the production were in the style of the dictator's Arab uniform. The king came on stage wearing a leg brace and a hunchback. Spacey commented that he was inspired by his observation of present-day politicians who deliberately manipulate the media to present a certain persona to the public, which is exactly how Charles the Second used the play. That being said, Spacey was ready to inject some comedy into the role, which, if he had been haunting the audience, Shakespeare might have appreciated. It is probable that The Bard, by his drawing of a manic and ridiculous caricature, was telling his audience not to take the story too seriously. Unfortunately, no matter how sophisticated we think we have become, many still do. The restoration playwright and wit, John Dryden, appointed Poet Laureate by King Charles the Second, observed this in his audiences too:

Some think the fools were most as times went then,
But now the world's o'er-stocked with prudent men.
...

This side today and that tomorrow burns;
So all are God a-mighties in their turns.
A tempting doctrine, plausible and new;
What fools our fathers were if this be true!

Earlier, back in 1984, Anthony Sher also played the king as a paraplegic, this time requiring a pair of crutches for support as he moved about the stage.

This was a gimmick, of course, as was Spacey's portrayal, though at least in Spacey's case the production was supposed to have a comedy element to it. The wonder is that nobody seems to have taken exception, which is unusual in the modern world.

Ian McKellen's Richard was another military fanatic, who enjoyed a good smoke. His King was a fascist and the play, set in the 1930's, was a reflective comment on the politics then. Of course, it was meant to serve as a warning to the modern world, which seems to have ignored it. What with a plethora of communication devices available to us, it seems the theatre has rather less influence on the public mind than of yore.

As for modern methods of communication, a new television version of Shakespeare's play has Sherlock Holmes in the title role while his sidekick, Doctor Watson, played the king on stage. Well, that is the actors who are famous for playing them on TV. Benedict Cumberbatch is Richard the Third in the new BBC2 series The Hollow Crown while Martin Freeman played the king on stage in a 2014 production at the Trafalgar Studios in London.

Cumberbatch is, according to a scientist at Leicester University, related to King Richard the Third, being his second cousin sixteen times removed. We might, thus, expect an empathic portrayal of the king, though Shakespeare's dialogue rather diverts any sympathy the actor might feel for perceived innocence in the character.

Freeman's portrayal spared us the graphic theatrical *props* of leg irons and crutches but relied on a traditional approach to acting where the king is crippled down one side. The set was a modern office and the dialogue took place over two rows of facing desks. The atmosphere recreated that of modern corporate conferencing, where opposing factions are facing each other, though separated by a space between.

Appendix 2 – More Ancient Bones

If there is one quality that can be truly said to be a common trait of humanity, it is the capacity for seduction by a plausible but false story. Some believe only the poorly educated or gullible can be readily fooled in this way, but the following examples show clearly that highly educated academics are among the easiest to deceive.

Piltdown Man

This story began back in 1912, not that long before the examination of the Westminster Bones. An amateur archaeologist named Charles Dawson claimed to have discovered fossilised remains of The Missing Link at Piltdown, Sussex, England. Dawson contacted Arthur Smith Woodward, Keeper of Geology at the National History Museum. Dawson was subtle. His first "find" was merely part of a skull, which he had found in gravel beds going back to the Pleistocene era. Dawson and Smith-Woodward began working the site together and soon "discovered" more artefacts – a set of teeth, a jawbone, skull fragments and even primitive tools which, they claimed, would have been used by what they were presenting as a single individual.

Smith-Woodward was influenced by the theory expressed famously by Charles Darwin that mankind had evolved from an ape-like creature. Fossils of the ape stage had been found, and also fossils of early humans, but there remained an evolutionary break – a missing link.

Archaeologists had been searching vainly for such a find and when Dawson presented his bones, the story got in the way of scientific analysis.

Smith-Woodward reconstructed a skull from the parts he and Dawson had found, which he and other archaeologists considered might be the elusive missing link. They suggested it was a human ancestor that had been living 500,000 years ago. Announcing their theory to the Geological Society in 1912, it was generally accepted by that august body of academics. The Missing Link had been found! Textbooks were rewritten to explain the intermediate characteristics of the new creature.

The famous writer, Arthur Conan Doyle got himself involved in the hoax, though as an inventor of fabulous tales he was perhaps the one most entitled to do so. It has been considered he was one who planted the fossils. He lived close to Piltdown village and published his novel "The Lost World" the year the Piltdown fossils were found. This was a story of dinosaurs and ape-men. Conan-Doyle believed in Spiritualism and was constantly mocked by the scientific establishment. Some have thought he might have been involved in the Piltdown hoax as a way of getting his revenge.

British scientists were so convinced Piltdown Man was the missing link they dismissed other, valid discoveries. In 1924, one Raymond Dart working in South Africa uncovered a fossil skull of what appeared to be an ape-man. It had human teeth, but its cranial cavity was much smaller than the Piltdown fossil and thus dismissed. Dart's find is now known as Australo-pithecines, or more commonly as Taung's Child. It eventually became properly recognised as part of the human family tree but at first was obscured as such by the Piltdown hoax.

Unlike the Westminster bones, however, with Piltdown Man there was no protective urn to secrete the remains away from prying eyes. In 1949 better technology was applied to test the age of the find and it was discovered the Piltdown remains were a mere 50,000 years old. By this time *Homo Sapiens* was well established so that disposed of the idea here was the missing link. This prompted further investigation and it soon became apparent, once a rational appraisal was made, that here were bones of two different species, the skull was human while the jaw was that of an orang-utan. Close examination of the teeth revealed they had been filed to make them resemble those of a human and the bones had been stained deliberately to match the conditions in the Piltdown gravel pits.

It had taken forty years to reveal the truth. In all that time the fanciful story of the Missing Link trumped intellectual debate. Those taken in were not a gullible public, fed with false information, but serious academics, who we might think, would have recognised the jawbone of an ape when they saw one and notice file marks on ape teeth. More analysis showed the skull to be of fairly recent origin and the other bones, though genuine fossils were from various parts of the world. All the bones of Piltdown Man had been deliberately planted. Had it not been for popular romance around the story of the missing link, Charles Dawson probably would not have thought to try it on.

The general public, though, have just as great a propensity for being deceived by a good story as academics. The American writer Samuel Clemens (Mark Twain), early in his career experimented with the public capacity for accepting a hoax, and surprised even himself at the result.

The Petrified Man

Samuel Clemens, after failing in his endeavours to become rich by working as a miner, talked his way into employment as a reporter for the Territorial Enterprise, a journal in Nevada. One of his first reports was of a petrified man discovered in the mountains of Nevada.

A stone mummy, a man petrified by ancient waters that had been dripping down upon him, was discovered in some mountains near a place called Gravelly Ford. He was sitting with his back to the rock and was completely whole except for his left leg, which was a false wooden one. He was estimated to have been there for a hundred years. His pensive attitude was indicated by the position of his right thumb, which rested by the side of his nose. The fore-finger pressed upon the corner of his eye to draw it half open while the right eye was closed and the fingers of the right hand were spread apart.

An inquest was called and the jury pronounced him deceased due to protracted exposure. The people of the area offered to give him a decent burial, but it was found he was fixed permanently to the rock by the limestone sediment that had petrified him. It was suggested he be blown clear with dynamite, but the local judge considered that would be sacrilege.

Clemens reported that over three-hundred people had visited the place to view the petrified man in the last five or six weeks. The story was taken up by other papers and circulated widely.

Not a word of it was true. In order to make a name for himself he invented a fantastic story intending to entertain his readers. He was surprised as to the numbers of people who believed it and admitted, later in life, to "a soothing secret satisfaction."

It was not as if there were no clues to the hoax. The position of the fingers of the right hand should have given the game away, and if not that, the suggestion of using explosive to get him off the mountain should have done it. According to Samuel Clemens, nobody discovered or comprehended the significant position of the petrified man's hands. It seems that when presented with a fanciful story, people fail to recognise that something is wrong even when obvious clues are put right under their noses.

The use of a wooden coffin by secret murderers comes somehow to mind.

The Curse of King Tut

The example of Samuel Clemen's work above brings to mind one of the most famous quotes attributed to him: "Never let the truth stand in the way of a good story, unless you can't think of anything better."

No doubt newspaper editors dusted down this aphorism and applied it to the story of the finding of Pharaoh Tutenkhamun by Howard Carter in 1922. The following year, as the story was losing it "legs", Lord Carnarvon, under whose financial auspices the expediton was being run, died in a Cairo hotel room. The cause was a mosquito bite that had delivered a bacterial infection, which, in the days before antibiotics, often proved fatal. Immediately it was reported he had fallen foul of King Tut's Curse, which stated that death would be visited upon anyone who violated his tomb. Newspapers were helped when around the time of his death, the lights in Cairo dimmed. This was a regular occurrence in that city but who other than the denizens of Cairo would know that?

It was claimed there was a curse written above the entrance to the tomb. There was, in fact, an inscription on the statue of a goddess, which was a standard spell from the Egyptian Book of the Dead intended to obtain eternal life

The story of King Tut's Curse was so potent films were made about it. A study conducted as late as 2002 and reported in The British Medical Journal concluded there was nothing to indicate the survival rate of those involved with the expedition of 1922 was any different to the rest of us. The story had been current then for eighty years. The whole thing was a hoax designed merely to sell newspapers.

A Japanese Paleolithic Hoax

A propensity for being hoaxed is not confined to the western world, nor to past generations. Here is one from the year 2000.

Certain paleolithic finds of the lower and middle periods were found in Japan by one of their most accomplished archaeologists, Shinichi Fujimura. He was working as Deputy Director for a private research centre. This time, though, the experts were not entirely taken in and rumours of fraud were leaking out. Journalists working for the Mainichi Shinbun newspaper got to hear of it and, going to a site where Fujimura was working, set up hidden surveillance cameras. He was caught planting artefacts on the site.

When confronted with the evidence, he was forced to confess to fraud.

What a pity there were no surveillance cameras at the Tower of London in 1674.

History Of Crowland

There is some uncertainty surrounding the identification of whoever wrote the Crowland Chronicle, which sets down details of the reign of King Richard the Third. Those parts written in the reign of Henry the Seventh are always going to be contentious, but the Abbey's earlier hoax hardly improves the integrity of Abbey writings.

In the year 1413, the Abbey at Crowland, situated in the Lincolnshire fens, claimed fraudulently lands belonging to another Abbey. In order to "prove" Crowland had tenure of these lands, a document was produced: *Historia Crowlandensis* (History of Crowland) giving documentary proof of the Abbey's ownership of the disputed lands. It was a number of ancient charters put together to assume the claim by Crowland. At the time it was accepted as genuine and the Abbey won its case.

The document gave a rare insight of the functioning of a medieval abbey and was thus accepted by later historians who perceived its value as a contemporary record. In the nineteenth century, certain historians began to suspect its veracity. There were things about it that were unreasonable. Claims were made that certain monks had studied at Oxford long before the university there was founded. Names of places and historical figures were mentioned using fourteenth-century terms including some that were supposed to be passages from the tenth century. Further study revealed details of bridge construction that was not developed at the time of the supposed writing. Several monks were claimed to be over a hundred years old; one achieved 148 years of age.

The document was a fake. The clues had been there all along but historians, being more interested in what they thought were contemporary examples of medieval life, which some might have been, for years failed to detect any fault.

These few examples show how much a good story influences the truth and actively prevents critical analysis of a historical event, even in those who would flatter themselves as being of the intellectual elite. Indeed, it is among these that historical fraud has most currency. The next time we read a history claiming to be a work of high scholarship, we might remind ourselves of that.

References

Please note that this list is not intended to be exhaustive, but provided as a convenience for anyone wishing to read more of the reign of King Charles the Second. There are so many works pertaining to the reign of King Richard the Third that only a selection is provided here.

Recent Investigations regarding the Fate of the Princes in the Tower
Lawrence E Tanner, Esq., M.V.O., M.A., F.S.A., and Professor William Wright, F.R.C.S., F.S.A.
Recollections of a Westminster Antiquary
Lawrence E Tanner
History of the Life and Reign of Richard the Third
James Gairdner
Richard III
Paul Murray Kendall
The Wars of the Roses
J. R. Lander
The Diary of Samuel Pepys
The Diary of John Evelyn
An Apology for the Royal Party (1659)
John Evelyn
A Journal of the Plague Year
Daniel Defoe
The History of King Richard III
Sir Thomas More

The English Princess, or the Death of Richard III
John Caryl
The King's Grave: The Search for Richard III
Philippa Langley and Michael Jones
The King's Revenge
Don Jordan & Michael Walsh
A Gambling Man: Charles II and the Restoration
Jenny Uglow

www.quoadultra.net

27767161R00061

Printed in Great Britain
by Amazon